Choose Your Lover
Carefully

Choose Your Lover Carefully

AN ASTROLOGICAL GUIDE

CASS & JANIE JACKSON

A Sterling / Zambezi Book
Sterling Publishing Co., Inc.
New York

Library of Congress Cataloging-in-Publication Data Available

2   4   6   8   10   9   7   5   3   1

Published in 2005 by Sterling Publishing Co., Inc.
387 Park Avenue South, New York, NY 10016
Text Copyright © 2005 Cass & Janie Jackson
Astrological drawings Copyright © 2005 Jonathan Dee
Published and distributed in the UK solely by
Zambezi Publishing Limited
P.O. Box 221 Plymouth,
Devon PL2 2YJ
www.zampub.com
Distributed in Canada by Sterling Publishing
$^{c}/o$ Canadian Manda Group, 165 Dufferin Street
Toronto, Ontario, Canada M6K 3H6
Distributed in Australia by Capricorn Link (Australia) Pty Ltd.
P.O. Box 704, Windsor, NSW 2756, Australia

Typesetting by Zambezi Publishing Ltd., Plymouth UK

For information about custom editions, special sales, premium and corporate
purchases, please contact Sterling Special Sales Department at 800-805-5489 or
specialsales@sterlingpub.com.

Zambezi ISBN: 1-903065-34-8
Sterling ISBN: 1-4027-2273-7

About the Authors

Cass Jackson was head of a large grammar school when he started to write. As a part-time freelance writer, he produced short stories for magazines and for boys' comics. At the same time, he was developing his interest in complementary therapies and new age subjects, eventually qualifying as a reiki master, herbalist, and astrologer. (He's also a registered goldsmith and silversmith!)

He quit teaching and became editor of a small automobile magazine. Cass also became director of studies for an international correspondence course on writing for children, and he produced several books on various aspects of writing. This led to several writing jobs, the launch of Cass and Janie's own magazine, and the establishment of residential courses.

Cass and Janie have written seven books on various mind, body, and spirit subjects and edited several more for various publishers. Both are astrologers and both are interested in healing, complementary health, and psychology.

Janie Jackson has worked in some form of writing and publishing all her life. She has worked on magazines and newspapers, either as staff, in public relations, or as a features writer. She has taught writing in adult education colleges, and along with Cass, she has run various courses for writers.

Dedication
To Lynne and Colin—who did.

Acknowledgment
Thank you to Jonathan Dee,
for designing the zodiac symbols in each chapter.

Contents

Introduction

Marriages, we're told, are made in heaven—but this institution appears to be going out of fashion in the twenty-first century. Judging from the number of marriages that end in disaster, it seems that heaven sometimes falls down on the job. However, whether you're looking for marriage or partnership, choosing a lover can be a tricky business. Where do you look for guidance? There are dozens of old wives' tales: Marry in haste, repent at leisure; Early brides make early deaths; and so on, but they're all pretty gloomy and often contradictory. Counseling is widely available, but this usually comes after you've made your choice and discovered your mistake.

Fortunately, there is a reasonably reliable system for choosing your mate. It's based on the theory that everything is "written in the stars." We're not talking here about the daily horoscope features that appear in magazines and newspapers and on the Internet, because choosing the right partner is much more important than wondering what sort of day you're going to have. Whether you're being pursued by innumerable would-be lovers or are unable to make up your mind about "old faithful," who has been around for years, you will find sound advice in this book that is based on the ancient theories of astrology—in addition to a few ideas from our own experiences as counselors.

Basic Facts About Astrology

To start with, of course, you will want to know something about how astrology works and how you can use it. Astrology is not a science, religion, cult, nor is it a Johnny-come-lately fad or fashion. It is knowledge that has existed for thousands of years. Scientists such as Isaac Newton and Galileo were also astrologers. Great generals—Napoleon, for instance—planned their campaigns with astrological assistance, and it is well known that several world leaders have depended heavily on advice from astrologers. In the East, astrology is an integral part of life, and even in the cynical West, thousands of people read their horoscopes every day.

You almost certainly know your Sun sign—that is, the sign of the zodiac covering the period in which you were born. Most people know, too, that for astrological purposes the year is divided into twelve sections, each represented by a certain sign.

The names given to these signs date back a long way, to the ancient civilizations of Egypt, Greece, and Rome. It is known that the Magi, the three wise men who searched for the Christ child, were astrologers, so convinced of the accuracy of their beliefs that they allowed a star to guide them. Until the seventeenth century, astrology was synonymous with astronomy. The ancient Greeks first established astrology as we now know it. The zodiac comprises the twelve constellations that lie along the apparent trajectory of the Sun around the Earth. Astronomers and astrologers call this pathway the ecliptic. We all know, of course, that the Earth orbits the Sun, but the ancients didn't understand this. Hence the use, even today, of phrases such as "The Sun is now entering the sign of Cancer" and so on. Stroll around a tree and notice how the view behind it changes as you walk. You will understand then the old idea that the Sun was moving through the signs and circling around the Earth.

The term "zodiac" derives from the word "zoo" and relates to the fact that certain constellations (groups of stars) look like animals or people—for example, the sign of the ram, bull, twins, crab and so on. We've all heard of Ursa Major (the Great Bear), Orion the Hunter, and many others. You may like to take a map of the stars outside with you on a clear, starry night to see how many of these constellations you can locate in the sky.

Sun Signs

In order to explain how astrology can help you to find the love of your life, we must first define the dates covered by each sign. The zodiac circle begins on March 21, which equates to the start of the ancient Roman year, and it starts with the sign of Aries. It then works its way through to the last sign, which is Pisces. Astrologers describe your birth sign as a "Sun sign" because the Sun was in Taurus, Gemini, or whatever sign, on the day you were born.

Astrological signs are always expressed in the same order, with Aries as the first sign of the zodiac and Pisces as the twelfth, but the date on which each sign starts changes a little from time to time. For example, although the first day of Aries is usually March 21, it can sometimes be on the twentieth. Although each new sign starts when the Sun appears to move into it, this movement does not occur at a set time or date every year. Thus, the dates that follow are average ones, similiar to the ones that appear in any newspaper or magazine horoscope column.

AVERAGE SUN SIGN DATES	
Aries	March 21 to April 19
Taurus	April 20 to May 20
Gemini	May 21 to June 21
Cancer	June 22 to July 22
Leo	July 23 to August 22
Virgo	August 23 to September 22
Libra	September 23 to October 22
Scorpio	October 23 to November 21
Sagittarius	November 22 to December 21
Capricorn	December 22 to January 20
Aquarius	January 21 to February 18
Pisces	February 19 to March 20

Born on the Cusp

Being born "on the cusp" may sound rather uncomfortable, but don't worry. It means only that you were born where one sign ends and another begins. If you're new to astrology, you may be confused, because some publications place you in one sign and some place you in another. There's an easy way to reach a decision about this. Simply surf the Internet using a search engine—such as www.Google.com—where you will find links to astrological Web sites such as www.sashafenton.com, with information about services that can provide you with an astrological chart. You'll be asked to give the place and date of birth for the person you're looking up, and—if possible—their time of birth. For the purposes of finding a Sun sign, it doesn't matter if you don't know the time of birth—just enter 12 noon.

Sun Sign Categories

First, look at the way the signs are divided up. Each fits into three different categories, known as genders, elements, and qualities.

The Genders

Each sign of the zodiac is either masculine or feminine. These descriptions have nothing to do with the sex of the person concerned. Some astrologers prefer the terms *positive* and *negative*; others refer to *yang* and *yin*. We use the standard astrological terms of *masculine* and *feminine* in this book. No matter how you choose to describe them, the signs alternate in the following order.

MASCULINE	FEMININE
(positive, yang, extrovert)	(negative, yin, introvert)
Aries	Taurus
Gemini	Cancer
Leo	Virgo
Libra	Scorpio
Sagittarius	Capricorn
Aquarius	Pisces

Masculine

Masculine-sign people are usually interested in what is going on in the world. They like to get around, they have a lot of friends, and they like making new ones. They're not highly emotional people and can take a detached, objective view of most circumstances.

Feminine

Feminine-sign people are generally very involved with their homes, families, and close friends. They are not much interested in "the outside world" and are more likely to be disturbed by domestic matters than by political events or world affairs.

As with everything in astrology, these descriptions are not written in stone, and you'll find that there are exceptions. Don't be surprised if you meet reserved and retiring Leos, outgoing Virgos, and lots of others who don't conform to type. There are reasons for such exceptions, but they belong to more advanced astrology books. One very useful book on such exceptions—also a Sterling/Zambezi book—is called *The Hidden Zodiac*.

The Elements

Each Sun sign also belongs to a second category, the elements, which are fire, earth, air, and water. These groupings mirror the energies fundamental to each Sun sign, as you will see below.

FIRE SIGNS	Aries, Leo, Sagittarius	Lively, forceful
EARTH SIGNS	Taurus, Virgo, Capricorn	Sensible, reserved
AIR SIGNS	Gemini, Libra, Aquarius	Outgoing, mentally alert
WATER SIGNS	Cancer, Scorpio, Pisces	Emotional, perceptive

Notice that all fire and air signs are extrovert (masculine), while the earth and water people are introvert (feminine).

Note: Despite the fact that the symbol for Aquarius is the water carrier, it is an air sign.

Fire Signs

All three of the fire signs—Aries, Leo, and Sagittarius—thrive on attention. They're positive, creative individuals who are full of enthusiasm, but be warned—they have a short fuse if they're stressed, tired, hungry, or unhappy, though this mood soon passes. If you're looking for an ardent lover, choose a fire sign.

Aries

Aries is a born leader whose motto could well be "Me first." These are the people who instinctively take charge of any situation, and few question their assumption of authority. They're usually very capable and decisive, but they may get bored if things don't move as quickly as they'd like them to.

Leo

Leo likes to be in charge but in a slightly different way from Aries. Leos are often found in managerial posts in large organizations. Their autocratic attitude gains respect from their subordinates, who are usually too dazzled by Leo's charisma to question his decrees.

Sagittarius

Sagittarians differ from the other two fire signs in that they tend to be less dictatorial. These people get what they want in more subtle ways. Often found as key figures in religious or educational situations, they are very concerned with the fate of the world—a trait they share with the air sign Aquarius. Philosophical Sagittarians can seem a bit aloof if you're looking for demonstrative affection, but they are well intentioned.

Earth Signs

The earth signs—Taurus, Virgo, and Capricorn—are probably the most levelheaded people in the zodiac. They adopt a realistic attitude to any situation and they are seldom fazed by emotional issues. This doesn't mean that they are cold or indifferent. On the contrary, when faced with any problem, they immediately adopt a down-to-earth approach to solving it. If you're seeking a lover who will look after you through thick and thin, choose an earth sign.

Taurus

Taurus is loyal, reserved, and attentive. Taurus lover's emotions run deep but are seldom shown, so don't expect them to make pretty speeches or write love poems. Taurus's particular talent lies in managing money and material resources. They won't run into debt and can be relied on to provide a comfortable family home, whatever their circumstances. Taurus partners won't often blow their tops but when they do—take cover!

Virgo

Virgos can be extremely introverted and are slow to voice emotional needs. These people are perfectionists, never accepting second best, and will spare no effort to live up to their own high standards. They will certainly expect you to do the same. Although probably financial wizards, Virgo lovers won't spend a fortune on glamorous gifts and expensive trips. They'll be too busy planning a secure future.

Capricorn

No matter what they undertake, Capricorns are capable operators. People born under this sign often head up a large and successful undertaking. Some of them prefer to have their own small business, which will run like clockwork. Capricorn partners will expect you to run their home with equal efficiency—and economy. They're not demonstrative, but if they are happy to be with you, they are reliable. If they are not entirely happy, they can keep an affair going outside the home for many years without you even being aware of it.

Air Signs

All the air signs—Gemini, Libra, and Aquarius—are intellectually bright in one way or another. They're sociable people, popular, and respected in business and in their private lives. Communication comes easily to them, so if you choose a partner born in an air sign, you'll never doubt their depth of devotion.

Gemini

Gemini has an original turn of mind and can often produce solutions to complicated problems. These people rely on plain facts and enjoy explaining them to others. They're inquisitive and will want to know all about you and your life, past and present, as soon as you meet. Gemini partners will probably talk too much, so you won't have a quiet life, but what they say is always worth hearing.

Libra

Librans come in several different types. Most of them are trustworthy, pleasant, and easygoing, but some can be lazy and reluctant to accept responsibility. This type can end up as a complete dropout. Others can be so ruthlessly ambitious that they're impossible to live with. If you choose a Libran lover, be careful to select the right type. That way, you'll have an agreeable, comfortable, if routine sort of life.

Aquarius

Aquarians are very concerned with the state of the world and humankind—but en masse rather than as individuals. They're very bright and love to discuss their ideals, but you may find their detachment something of a problem. They won't hesitate to break a date with you if a peace rally or something similar claims their attention. Aquarians are exciting lovers, if you can cope with their unconventional lifestyle and unpredictability.

Water Signs

Most of the water signs—Cancer, Scorpio, and Pisces—can be highly intuitive or even psychic to some degree. All three are intensely emotional and sensitive, though they display these qualities in different ways. They're devoted to their families and friends, but still expect to have their own way most of the time. In fact, some water signs can be extremely demanding—and you may find your watery partner too possessive for your taste.

Cancer

Cancer characters are easily hurt, and they tend to brood darkly about real or imagined slights. They make much of their devotion to their families, but they can often be extremely selfish—a fact that they deny hotly. These people are shrewd cookies who have a clear idea of the value of money and material possessions. If you take a Cancerian lover, be prepared to cope with mood swings. They easily become depressed—but a little TLC and flattery can soon coax them around.

Scorpio

Scorpio natives are deep thinkers, imaginative, and intuitive. Once they make up their minds about anything, they're unlikely to budge. They won't argue, but neither will they accept defeat. They'll just bide their time to achieve their aims. At the same time, these people are sensitive and helpful to others. Scorpio partners may not be easy to live with, but any misfortune will bring out the best in them.

Pisces

Pisces could well be described as the most watery of all the signs. People born under this sign are intensely emotional and tend to drift aimlessly from one relationship to another. Somehow, the cake in the bakery window always seems more appealing than the one they already have. Pisces subjects are excitable and can be secretive, but they're determined people not easily distracted from their chosen path. Choose a Pisces partner and your life could well be chaotic or a series of dramas—but it will never be dull.

The Qualities

The three qualities—cardinal, fixed, and mutable—represent the last of the divisions. See the chart on top of the next page.

CARDINAL	FIXED	MUTABLE
Aries (fire)	Taurus (earth)	Gemini (air)
Cancer (water)	Leo (fire)	Virgo (earth)
Libra (air)	Scorpio (water)	Sagittarius (fire)
Capricorn (earth)	Aquarius (air)	Pisces (water)

Cardinal Signs

Traditionally, those born in a cardinal sign are supposed to be the self-starters of the zodiac, the people who come up with all the bright ideas. We're not too sure about this. We've often noticed that if a cardinal sign comes up with a brilliant scheme, he leaves it to others to put his ideas into practice. All four signs within this group do like to be the center of attention, but they achieve their aims in different ways.

Aries is always at the front of the line, Cancer gets what he or she wants in more roundabout ways, Libra uses his or her charm to good effect, and Capricorn just keeps plodding along. However, whatever method they use, each of the cardinal signs usually manages to get his or her way in the end.

These people are totally convinced that no matter what needs to be done, their way is the best. You may employ tact, sweet reason, wiles, or temper tantrums, but they remain convinced that they are right. Even if they appear weak in some way—financially, emotionally, or health wise—they use their apparent handicaps to manipulate any situation to their advantage. However, cardinal signs have one outstanding virtue—they inspire others to greater achievements.

Fixed Signs

It will come as no surprise to learn that fixed-sign people tend to be set in their ways and often very stubborn.

Taurus is possibly the most unyielding of the fixed signs, Leo tends to be vain but is tremendously determined, Scorpio is outstandingly tenacious, inclined to persevere rather than give up, and Aquarius can be a little overbearing in his or her efforts to maintain the status quo.

Fixed-sign people are the ones who endure a bad marriage or a job they dislike for far too long, simply because they hate change and like to see any undertaking through to the finish. They may agonize and moan for years but do nothing about it. However, when the end comes—and it invariably does—they will make drastic changes quickly and suddenly. Sometimes, they simply walk out— and nothing will induce them to reconsider their decision. They've had enough and often go on to make a completely new life for themselves. If you choose a lover from a fixed sign, remember not to push him or her too far.

Mutable Signs

Mutable-sign people tend to be versatile and changeable. They're very difficult to understand and can be indecisive.

Gemini can talk his or her way into or out of any situation, Virgo hates to be pressured, Sagittarius tends to exaggerate everything, and Pisces can be moody and oversensitive.

Mutable signs find it difficult to be decisive about anything. They all believe that variety is the spice of life, and they love to be on the move. New experiences, places, jobs, and people are essential to them. If you take a lover from one of the mutable signs, don't expect your lover to be faithful. Mutable-sign people mean what they say at the time that they say it—but that was yesterday. Accuse them of unreliability and, true to their mutable tendencies, they'll talk their way out of it. Life with the mutable signs may be erratic, but it's never boring.

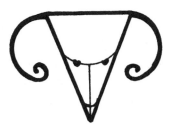

Aries

March 21 to April 20

Gender: *Masculine/Extrovert*
Element: *Fire*
Quality: *Cardinal*
Ruling Planet: Mars

On the day that you were born, the Sun was in the fire sign Aries, the first of the zodiac. You are therefore a force to be reckoned with—a masculine cardinal sign ruled by the planet Mars and with the ram as its symbol. If you have any enemies, they will find you a potent and determined adversary.

Aries Characteristics

Your greatest objective in life is to win. You hate to lose, whether you're playing tiddlywinks with your grandchildren or you're involved in a multimillion-dollar deal.

Aries is the sign of new beginnings. You're a great organizer, but others may think you egotistical, constantly rushing in to take charge. You feel compelled to complete any job at full speed and at all costs, but if you don't get the results you want, you'll stop leading and start delegating. In other words, you'll leave all the dirty work to your subordinates, and move on to new pastures.

What You Look Like

Ariens are usually of medium height and build. Mars is your ruling planet and you're extremely active, so you may be one of the fortunate few who don't put on weight as you get older. However, some Aries people do gain weight because they love to cook and eat desserts, cakes, and cookies. Whatever your race, and regardless of your basic skin color, you're likely to have a reddish or bronzed appearance, with thick hair and deep-set eyes.

You probably love buying expensive new clothes, whether you can afford them or not. Most Ariens are very concerned about the image they project to the world and so love to spend money on their clothes and appearance. You may not store your clothes properly or change before doing a messy job, so you throw more serviceable clothes away than most other zodiac types do. Anyway, ruining a garment gives you a wonderful excuse to buy something new.

Some Ariens are extremely good-looking. Even if you're not, you are likely to be attractive because of your lively attitude and the cheerful smile that is never far from your face.

Aries in Love

You have a truly awesome capacity for concentration, and this can be one of your greatest assets. However, as a true Arien, you will never be so single-minded that you don't have time for amorous distractions. On the contrary, you will probably break quite a few hearts before you settle down, and you will almost certainly form some short-lived but sexy relationships.

Ariens are more likely than most to fall head-over-heels in love when the right partner comes along. Don't allow your passionate, impulsive nature to draw you into an affair that is more lust than love. Consult the stars before entering into any commitment.

You will probably fall in love a thousand times before you decide to settle down. When this does happen, you will be steadfast, reliable, and faithful. In return, you'll expect your partner to be waiting with open arms when you come home. This doesn't mean that you'll want to put on your slippers and watch television, because you'll want to whisk your partner off to some new adventure.

Typically, you're impulsive and impatient; these qualities are sure to affect any partnership you may form. You like to lead, you can be assertive or even aggressive in your approach, and you expect your partner to follow. You are unable to understand why your partner can't see things the way that you do. You're not above using some rather dubious tactics to get your own way—on the premise that the ends justify the means. Reason and diplomacy are foreign to you.

Your zest for life is considerable, and woe betide anyone who tries to put out that fire. You jump at the opportunity to try anything fresh and interesting, even if it's only going to a new restaurant for dinner. Your inability to accept advice is one of those down points that occasionally lead you into trouble, but it's no good telling you that—you're not listening.

Your Career

Most Ariens work for large organizations, often schools. You have a natural love of words and language, which could lead to a career in writing, advertising, or public relations. Some Ariens are politically adroit, an aptitude that serves them in good stead in any type of business. You're at your best when you are doing the organizing and everything is going smoothly. Typically, Ariens are exceptionally capable and never hesitate to take on the most daunting assignments.

Your Health

As far as your health is concerned, you are a strange mixture. You will endure serious illness and intense pain without a murmur, yet get quite worked up about a slight cut or some minor ailment.

Aries rules the head, which includes the brain. You, more than any other Sun sign, are likely to suffer from migraines. Be aware of the possibility of head injuries, caused through accident or your own negligence. As luck would have it, you will be the one to suffer a blow to the head if you're not wearing your hard hat when caving, climbing, riding, or even working. You have been warned! More Ariens fall on their heads than land on their feet.

Stress is usually something you take in your stride, but be careful because Ariens do sometimes succumb to stress-related ailments and even mental problems. Take heart, because if you do become sick, your positive approach to life will ensure that you will cope with illness much better than the bearers of other signs.

What You Look for in a Partner

Because no Arien suffers fools gladly, you need a partner whose intelligence will match your own. Patience and a tolerant nature will be essential if that partner is to cope with your impulsive, and sometimes erratic, behavior. On the rare occasions that you're feeling depressed or unwell, you'll expect understanding and sympathy in abundance—plus more practical consolation, like a double Scotch and a cool hand on your fevered brow.

Demonstrative affection is essential to you, and you will certainly demand fireworks in the bedroom. In fact, the sex life of many Ariens continues well into old age, depending, of course, on an equally sensual partner.

Three Compatible Signs

Gemini

Gemini is the sign most likely to be compatible with Aries. Geminis will never bore you and will always be supportive and encouraging when you get yet another brilliant idea. On the rare occasions when you feel in the doldrums, they will probably suggest an interesting or exciting outing to divert you.

Do realize, though, that your Gemini lover will probably be a worrier who will obsess about things that you consider quite trivial. Overall, an Aries-Gemini relationship has a lot going for it and is likely to be highly successful.

Aquarius

Aquarius has lots of common sense, and that's a quality you may lack to some degree. These people also have a good sense of humor—and, let's face it—anybody living with Aries must be able to see the funny side of life. Your Aquarian partner is unlikely to bore you, because you'll never know what he or she is going to do next. You may not find this so amusing, though, when your partner suddenly spends the mortgage money on a designer dress or an expensive car. Their concern for humanity en masse may cause a few disagreements because you'd prefer them to concentrate solely on you. Aquarians like their own way, and if they don't get it, they can resort to hurtful sarcasm. The Aries-Aquarius relationship is likely to be somewhat tempestuous but, with goodwill on both sides, it can be successful.

Pisces

Your Pisces partner will be a true romantic and is likely to live in a fantasy world, so don't expect this individual to share your concern with the realities of life. Pisces women are most definitely not domestic goddesses. Their homes tend to be chaotic, but their loving nature and unfailing loyalty more than compensate for erratic mealtimes and unmade beds. They need their own space and can be secretive. When they're deeply involved in some fantasy or another—on television, in a book, or even in their own mind—they'll expect you to cope with the chores and leave them alone. Overall, an Aries-Pisces partnership can be surprisingly successful. It just needs a fair bit of give and take—though who does the giving and who the taking is difficult to define.

Where to Find Your Partner

Geminis have many interests, but they're not very keen on hard work. They love to pass on information, so you may find them as a reporter for your local paper, in a law office, as a teacher, or even at a tourist information bureau. They're clever with their hands, so look for them at craft clubs or evening classes. They're talkative, so debating societies or amateur dramatics may appeal to them. Nevertheless, Gemini people are so changeable that you could find them almost anywhere.

Aquarians are never happier than when they are helping other people. Find them in any charitable concern or even in refugee camps. An Aquarian could be a psychologist, a radiographer, or a social worker. They often use writing, broadcasting, or publishing as a means of expressing their ideals. You'll find your partner in any situation involving other people, particularly when they need support. They're almost certain to be involved with some sort of voluntary organization.

Pisceans are not particularly ambitious people, so you're unlikely to find your partner in a high-pressure job. This sign's tendency to moodiness and romanticism means that accepting responsibility is alien to them. They're crazy about animals, so you may find your lover as an assistant to a vet or at a dog show. They love flowers, so look for them in a florist's shop or at flower shows. Pisceans have definite psychic tendencies so could belong to various esoteric groups and clubs. They also love water, so you could meet them at a swimming pool or the seaside.

How to Please Your Lover

Your Gemini partner loves the old-fashioned flowers, like lavender and lily-of-the-valley. Your lover will almost certainly be delighted with similarly perfumed toiletries or plants for the garden. A Gemini is a great one for gadgets in the office and the kitchen. Clothes are important to Gemini but, before you buy them, make sure that your choice will coordinate with the colors of your partner's existing wardrobe. Geminis are likely to favor all shades of yellow, and the agate is their birthstone.

Aquarians love antiques—the genuine article, not a reproduction, however good it may be. If you really want to impress your partner, give him or her your grandmother's aquamarine ring because this pale blue gem is the Aquarian's birthstone. Aquarians will be grateful for gifts of books, but make sure they haven't already read the one you choose. They'll also appreciate a donation to their favorite charity. Given a choice of flowers, they'll almost certainly opt for orchids. They'll be delighted with an unusual gift, and in fact, anything different will please Aquarians, as long as it's good-quality. They'll scorn anything cheap and trashy.

True to their spiritual outlook, Pisces partners could be delighted with a visit to a stone circle or a haunted house. They love flowers and plants, too, particularly those that grow near water, and will probably be delighted if you present them with a kitten or a puppy. Ask first, though, just in case they're allergic to animal dander; perhaps a goldfish in a bowl would be safer. Take them to a séance or a talk on one of the mind-body-spirit subjects. Arrange for them to see a clairvoyant or have a tarot reading. Their birthstone is the delicate moonstone.

Taurus

April 20 to May 20

Gender: *Feminine/Introvert*
Element: *Earth*
Quality: *Fixed*
Ruling Planet: *Venus*

On the day that you were born, the Sun was in the earth sign Taurus, the second sign of the zodiac. This is a fixed sign, indicating a strong and stable personality. Taurus, a feminine sign, is ruled by the planet Venus, the goddess of love, ensuring that you are one of life's romantics. The symbol for Taurus is the bull—an apt emblem for you, as you share several of the animal's characteristics.

Taurus Characteristics

Taureans are probably the most persistent characters of the zodiac, so whatever your goal, you will never relax until you achieve it. This may be the reason that so many people regard you as stubborn. Before coming to any decision, you will spend some time in thought, and even then, you won't be in any hurry to do anything. You will take action when you are ready and not before.

Security and stability are essential to you. It is this need for security that makes you buy so many luxury items. Once you have what you want, nothing will induce you to give it up. That applies right across the board, from material possessions to relationships.

You dislike change of any kind, and it takes you a long time to become accustomed to it.

What You Look Like

Taureans are usually sturdy and of medium height. Because you tend to be lazy and love to eat, your weight could be an ongoing problem. Counter this by doing lots of strenuous exercise. You probably have small hands and feet and move quite gracefully. Undoubtedly, and whatever your race, your most striking feature will be your beautiful, soft eyes. This feature, with your gentle expression and quiet manner, can make you extremely attractive.

Your taste in clothes is simple and elegant. Typically, you buy the most expensive that you can afford, and they last you a long time. You like the earth colors, browns (particularly golden russet toncs) and greens, and these suit you well.

Taurus in Love

Taurus never rushes into anything, particularly where affairs of the heart are concerned. You're often reluctant to show your feelings, and love at first sight is definitely not for you. Your worst scenario would be to be let your guard down, and you are very cautious about the mating game. This hesitation can be misunderstood. Be careful that it is not mistaken for complete lack of interest.

Once you're sure of your feelings (and of your lover) you will enter into a passionate and enduring relationship, and thereafter you will remain devoted to your partner. Even then, you show your love by actions rather than words because you find communication difficult. Because you're clever with money, you will be able to provide a comfortable and beautiful home for your family—and they will certainly be well fed. Taurus is usually too reserved to play the field as far as suitors are concerned. If you have been hurt in the past, you'll be suspicious about new relationships, and this could make you reluctant to show your feelings.

Although it's usually well hidden, you do have a rather jealous nature. You can also be deeply hurt, often because you have misconstrued somebody's words or actions. This can lead to a display of Taurean rage, a rare but alarming experience. Instead of voicing your fury, make a big effort to say those three little words that you find so difficult to utter—*I love you.*

Your Career

Taureans have a valuable and innate ability to handle money. A career in banking or some other aspect of finance would suit you well. Your infinite patience and compassion also mean that any position in which you are able to help other people will give you great satisfaction. Some Taureans are drawn to the music industry, while others are attracted to agriculture and farming. Whichever vocation you choose, success is important to you, and you will work extremely hard to achieve it. This trait is invaluable to your employers and, as a result, your reliability will be much appreciated.

Your Health

Overall, Taureans are hardy. They don't worry about their health until something goes wrong. When that happens, they seek medical help.

Taurus rules the neck and throat. You may well have an excellent singing voice, but you might also be prone to sore throats. A stiff neck and even accidents to the neck may be common complaints. Tonsillitis may plague you at certain times of the year, especially if you are in a profession where you use your voice a lot. Taurean teachers are particularly prone. There is an old wives' tale that female Taureans are terrible gossips—hence their frequent throat troubles. If the shoe fits … Laryngitis, swollen neck glands, and even thyroid problems are a possibility. Take care of your teeth, too. Dental problems are another Taurean weakness.

What You Look for in a Partner

Above all else, Taurus needs a loyal and supportive partner. Your inborn determination means that you can cope with almost anything fate throws at you, providing your partner is always clearly on your side. Your tendency to be obstinate could cause problems if the other person in your life is equally stubborn. Taureans love money and what it brings, so it would be great if your partner happened to be wealthy. If that's not possible, you need someone who recognizes the value of money and isn't extravagant. You have an extremely sensual nature and need a mate who will match your ardor. You prefer the other person to make the first move, because you're inclined to be shy. All Taureans are devoted to their families, so your lover should just adore your mom, dad, brothers, sisters, and so on. You look for a partner who is happy to make a nice home and to enjoy family life. This said, you are extremely sociable, so company is welcomed. You love the opportunity to go out and have a good time, so you need a partner who is comfortable in all kinds of social situations.

Three Compatible Signs

Taurus

Your most compatible partner is likely to be another Taurus. You will understand each other perfectly, happily building your lives on typically Taurean values. Arguments are unlikely because you will both be working toward the same objectives.

However, there could be a downside to all this sweetness and light. You're both stubborn, and if, by any chance, you should find yourselves in competition over anything, it's unlikely that either of you will give in. That's when the fireworks could go off in a double display of Taurean fury. Bear this in mind and your Taurus-Taurus partnership could work remarkably well.

Libra

Libra has a well-developed sense of fair play, and this will work well with your need for security. This will be an affectionate, kindly relationship. You are both ruled by the planet Venus, which encourages companionship as well as a loving sexual relationship.

Libra's laid-back attitude appeals to Taurus, who hates to be pressured or rushed in any way.

One slight cause of disagreement could be Libra's untidiness. You may find this irritating because you love an immaculate home. However, if you gently mention this, your easygoing Libra will make great efforts to improve. In fact, the art of compromise is something that you, a stubborn Taurus, could learn from your Libran partner. A Taurus-Libra relationship may not be world-shaking, but it should be successful.

Capricorn

It's likely that you will meet your Capricorn partner through business. Neither of you believes in love at first sight, so there's no risk that you will be swept off your feet. What begins as an office friendship may slowly develop into something deeper. Once committed, Capricorn will be completely faithful, but don't expect passionate declarations of undying love. In fact, Taurus is usually the more demonstrative partner in this relationship.

Capricorn can be extremely critical and will expect everything in the home to run like clockwork. Like Taurus, these people are persevering and patient. You're both earth signs and have your feet firmly on the ground, so a Taurus-Capricorn pairing is likely to be a good one.

Where to Find Your Partner

Since you are a Taurus, you won't have to look far for your most compatible partner. Taureans are very practical people and excel at do-it-yourself projects. You could find each other in clubs or classes dealing with cooking, gardening, or other hands-on activities. Take a vacation on a farm, attend an art class, or learn about hairdressing, beauty treatments, and special-effect cosmetics in a like-minded group. Keep your eyes open for the right person when you go to the opera or learn to play a musical instrument. Make friends, too, with your bank manager or accountant—both have the financial shrewdness that is so important to you.

Librans are always happy to help others, and they like to work as part of a team or in a partnership. Their well-balanced outlook means that you could find a Libran working as a lawyer, in real estate, or as a human resources manager. You won't find Librans in factories or anywhere else that is noisy and dirty. Their well-developed aesthetic sense means they are attracted to careers in hairdressing, the beauty business, or fashion. You may find your partner at an art gallery or in a poetry group. Librans gravitate to any situation that demands harmony and a well-balanced attitude.

Capricorns are good for serious Taurus because they make you laugh. This is a priceless asset if hard times come along. These people are materially minded, which blends well with your Taurean urge for possessions. You will almost certainly find your Capricorn lover holding a responsible position in a business or commercial enterprise. Capricorns tend to gravitate toward publishing or banking, but they can also be found running their own businesses with great efficiency.

Like Taurus, Libra is an earth sign, and you may meet you lover in a group associated with "green" issues, running a health food store, or even in a political organization.

How to Please Your Partner

You should find it easy to please your Taurus partner because you have so much in common. If you buy your partner flowers, you will confidently offer lilies, chrysanthemums, or foxgloves because you both like them so much. Your partner will share your passion for quality items of any kind, but will be particularly grateful for anything that enhances the comfort and beauty of the home. Emerald is your birthstone, so this is the gem that you should choose.

If your lover is a Libran, he or she will appreciate any gifts that are either beautiful or designed to enhance their looks. Both sexes like bric-a-brac of all kinds, but particularly antique jewelry. If it happens to include jade or sapphires, so much the better. Less expensively, Libra will be delighted by the gift of a basket of berries you have picked yourself. Because you are both ruled by Venus, you will share a taste for big, bold, and beautiful flowers, like roses, hydrangea, and poppies.

Capricorn, too, loves flowers, but likes pansies better than the large, showy blooms. Capricorns prefer silver to gold, and their birthstone is the turquoise, which looks best when set in silver. Because your Capricorn lover adores music, he or she will be delighted with concert tickets, or the latest recording of a favorite orchestra or group. Although these people are no gourmets, they do enjoy a good meal. They love pasta, so perhaps a visit to an Italian restaurant would be a good idea. Don't go overboard with expensive gifts for your Capricorn partner. You'll probably be accused of wasting money!

Gemini

May 21 to June 21

Gender: Masculine/Extrovert
Element: Air
Quality: Mutable
Ruling Planet: Mercury

On the day that you were born, the Sun was in the air sign of Gemini, the third sign of the zodiac. This is a mutable sign, indicating your flexibility and dislike of routine. Gemini, a masculine sign, is ruled by the planet Mercury—the messenger of the gods. The metal mercury is also known as quicksilver, which is appropriate for Gemini, as you act and think quickly. The symbol for Gemini is the twins, indicative of your decidedly dual personality.

Gemini Characteristics

One useful aspect of this duality is that you can do, or think about, two different things at the same time. You may even juggle two occupations. This seems perfectly natural to you, but you do tend to jump from one thing to another. Your friends probably say that you have a grasshopper mind. However, moving on to something else doesn't mean that you have forgotten all about the first topic.

Gemini is never at a loss for words. In fact, conversation is one of your favorite pastimes. Here you use gossip, laced with wit, irony, and exaggeration to mask your lack of confidence. Another problem for you could be your inability to reach a decision—it's as if the twins are pulling you in different directions. Your nervous energy keeps you always on the move, and you are essentially adaptable and versatile.

What You Look Like

As a Gemini, you are likely to look much younger than your actual age. Whatever your race, you will be slim and agile. Coloring varies according to race, but mousy hair may bother you. Why not cash in on your duality and have blond or silver streaks applied? You usually take great care of your hands, but you tend to nibble your nails if you're under stress—which happens more often than you care to admit.

Although your weight is not usually a problem in your younger years, be careful not to become obese as you grow older. Clothes are important to you and you always look elegant, preferring formal wear to the more casual look. Your chosen colors for clothing or decor will be yellow and light blue.

Gemini in Love

One decidedly regrettable result of your twofold Gemini nature is that you are quite likely to jump from one partner to another, thereby earning a reputation for flirtatiousness. This makes for difficult relationships. With your quick wit, you easily attract others, but you find it difficult to maintain any liaison, partly because you seldom trust anybody. What's more, you don't trust your own emotions and find it hard to express them.

It is in your nature to let your head rule your heart, which is seldom the best way to establish any form of relationship. You can talk yourself out of any situation but you find it much more difficult to talk yourself into a permanent partnership. This may be because while others are charmed by your wit and smart talk, they tend to see you as being rather superficial.

Geminis like to have a second string to their bow in practically any partnership and are not above two-timing. You are so changeable that you can easily become bored with a lasting one-to-one relationship. Eventually, though, you will meet your soul mate and may even overcome your fickle nature. Whether or not you are able to be very faithful remains to be seen.

Your Career

Your ruling planet, Mercury, makes Geminis the communicators of the zodiac. The teaching profession is ideally suited to you, and this could be linked with some of your other talents, such as design, arts and crafts, and music. If teaching is not for you, there are several alternatives. You're probably a computer whiz kid and could do well in an IT career. Your flair for words makes you an excellent interviewer, which opens up careers in radio and television, employment agencies, human resources, or reporting. All forms of transport appeal to you because you like to be constantly on the move. However, flitting from one job to another doesn't look good on your resume, so opt for a profession that offers a great deal of the variety you need.

Your Health

Some Geminis are fortunate and never seem to get ill. Others may suffer from problems with the shoulders, arms, and hands. The extremely painful condition known as frozen shoulder and another that is known as RSI (repetitive strain injury) often assault natives of this sign, so try not to spend too long at a keyboard. Beware, too, of tennis elbow, which can occur suddenly and for no apparent reason.

Gemini colds tend to settle in the chest and can therefore give rise to some nasty infections affecting the lungs. Asthma can be another problem in this area. Gemini, of all the signs, should not smoke, but unfortunately some do, quite heavily. This is probably due to their high-strung nature. In fact, it's possible that nerves are at the root of most Gemini maladies.

What You Look for in a Partner

Lighthearted, changeable Geminis need a partner who can cope with their erratic qualities. In general, people born under this sign are not that good at long-term relationships, and sadly, divorce is quite common among them. Your partner needs to be forgiving, good-tempered, flexible, understanding, placid—and then some! Patience, too, will be needed to cope with restless, chattering Gemini. Such paragons are in short supply, so it may well be that you will need to alter your own habits in order to establish a lasting relationship.

Three Compatible Signs

Aries

Aries is without doubt your most compatible partner. In this relationship, you'll both be full of bright ideas and exciting plans for the future. Neither of you can tolerate boredom, so you'll both enjoy exploring the grass on the other side of the fence.

You're both highly sexed, which will be another plus to this relationship. Ariens need demonstrative affection, too, particularly when they're depressed. You'd be well advised to learn to express sympathy at such times (even if you don't feel it.) However, don't expect sympathy or understanding when you're on one of your worrying binges, as this aspect of your nature will irritate Aries. A Gemini-Aries partnership may be stormy at times, but it can succeed remarkably well.

Virgo

Virgo's ruling planet, like your own, is Mercury so this should ensure that there's no lack of communication in your relationship. You both have a lively intelligence, though Virgo may find it tricky to keep up with that grasshopper mind of yours. Virgo is a perfectionist and you may find this irritating, particularly when it concerns your somewhat happy-go-lucky approach to housekeeping. Physically and emotionally, you are well matched, since you're both quite sexy yet find demonstrative affection difficult.

A Gemini-Virgo partnership could work well, as long as you both come down to earth at times and discuss the realities of life.

Aquarius

Aquarius and Gemini are both somewhat cool and detached, though in different ways. You have much in common intellectually, but this is not a highly emotional relationship. Aquarius is more concerned with humanity as a whole than with individuals, and Gemini tends to look elsewhere for admiration. However, since neither sign is possessive or jealous, these attitudes don't necessarily militate against a successful partnership.

You both need your own space and, in this pairing, usually get it. That being so, the Aquarius-Gemini relationship could be detached and unusual, but surprisingly rewarding.

Where to Find Your Partner

Aries enjoys physical activity and will almost certainly belong to a number of sports clubs. Ariens enjoy working with people, so you may find them in youth clubs or other social and community activities. Any energetic pursuit will appeal to them, so you'll almost certainly find an Aries at the gym, gardening, climbing mountains, or in some type of military activity. They also appreciate the arts, so they can be found at art exhibitions, in local dramatic societies, or in musical organizations.

Virgoans believe in service to the community, so you'll find them in charitable organizations or in the medical world. If you're unfortunate enough to land in the hospital, you'll probably find that your lovely doctor or sympathetic nurse is a Virgo. They're particularly interested in complementary therapies and remedies and make excellent counselors. Despite their innate reserve, Virgo natives love to act. They may work in the theater or appear in amateur productions. Look for them in any hobby or profession that permits self-expression.

Aquarius, too, enjoys working with other people, but quite often you'll find that they do this through running their own small business. You're more likely to find your partner running the corner store or a small boutique than in a large organization. They make good teachers, too, and can often be found as evening class tutors. Their concern for other people can lead them into paid or voluntary social services. They take their hobbies very seriously—and those pastimes can be extremely varied, from making matchstick models to studying astronomy or quantum physics.

How to Please Your Lover

Aries loves diamonds, and if you have jewelry in mind, these are the stones to buy—but be sure they're set in gold. Most Ariens enjoy cooking, so they will be delighted with gifts for the kitchen. They'll also enjoy being taken out for a meal, particularly to an Italian or Indian restaurant, as they enjoy hot, strong-tasting food. Ariens love to be noticed, and this applies to their taste in flowers. They're not interested in anything small and delicate, so huge red roses or golden sunflowers will be more to their taste.

Virgoans enjoy receiving gifts of any kind but are sometimes too reserved to express their gratitude. Unlike Ariens, they love small flowers, the more brightly colored the better, but they particularly like buttercups and forget-me-nots. It's not easy to buy gifts for this sign, and sometimes a gift certificate enabling them to make their own choice is the safest bet. A surprising number of Virgoans are vegetarians. Most of them love animals, so they'll appreciate a donation to an animal charity or even a gift for their own pet.

Aquarius is likely to be an avid collector of antiques, large or small. This means that finding a suitable gift is relatively easy, because your lover will be as delighted with a Victorian thimble as with a Georgian bookcase. These people pride themselves on their good taste, so avoid reproductions of any kind. Good watercolors or oil paintings will please them, but they must be originals. They'll be grateful, too, for antiquarian books.

Cancer

June 22 to July 22

Gender: *Feminine/Introvert*
Element: *Water*
Quality: *Cardinal*
Ruling Planet: *The Moon*

On the day that you were born, the Sun was in the water sign of Cancer, the fourth sign of the zodiac. As a water sign, your ruling planet is the Moon. These two factors combine to make you a rather deeper person than you appear to be. Cancer is also a cardinal sign, making you extremely creative and imaginative. The symbol for Cancer is the crab, which describes you to a tee: hard on the surface but with a soft interior, and with claws that can give a nasty nip.

Cancer Characteristics

Like the crab that walks sideways, you avoid tackling problems head-on because you prefer to sidetrack them. This caution is obvious, too, when you are introduced to strangers. You keep your distance until you are confident about them, and then you absorb them into all aspects of your life, taking care of your friends just as you look after your family. You often have an instinctive understanding of children.

You're apt to be moody—on cloud nine one minute and down in the dumps the next, a tendency that makes you hard to understand. Try to control this, because it makes you difficult to live with. True to your cardinal quality, you strike out in the direction you think best and you are not easily deflected from your path. Whatever project engages your attention, you want to be in charge and you resent interference. Don't let your unyielding exterior (your shell) prevent you from seeking advice when you need it. Admit that, just occasionally, you don't know best, and avoid wrecking a valuable venture.

You're a shrewd person and have an exceptionally retentive memory, though you're apt to allow your emotions to color your thoughts. You may also be interested in the occult and particularly impressionable to psychic influences.

What You Look Like

Cancerians come in two types. The first is of medium height, with a tendency toward plumpness, and often has thick, dark brown hair. The second type may be small and thin, with red hair and blue eyes. Most Cancer subjects, regardless of race or color, have clear, smooth skin and lustrous hair. And finally—a beauty hint. Some Cancerians tend to worry about everything. Be warned that this could have a disastrous effect on your looks, causing frown lines, a down-turned mouth, and a miserable expression.

Cancer is not overly concerned about appearances, but always manages to look well groomed and elegant in simple, good-quality clothes. You are drawn to all the Moon colors, silvery gray and blue, and you tend to stick to them in dress and decor.

Cancer in Love

Love is something of a Cancer pastime. You're an attractive person and will have no difficulty in finding admirers. All's well to start with and you thoroughly enjoy that first fine careless rapture, until you realize that a love affair makes demands on both partners. You're not so keen on that, and you will probably withdraw unless your lover happens to be the one.

You tend to hide your emotions, but you're a romantic at heart. You long to find that perfect someone with whom you can have a long-term relationship. If you're a woman, you'll be subconsciously looking for a father for your children. If you're a man, you may be seeking a mother figure. Sometimes you tend to rush into a relationship, but because you need security, you'll usually hold back until you are sure of yourself and your would-be partner.

Despite your instinctive caution about choosing a lover, you're always reluctant to end a relationship. You won't want to let them go, even if they have passed their expiration date and forgotten your birthday. This highlights the possessive streak in your nature, something to be controlled and concealed as much as possible. It's not endearing.

Your Career

The most suitable careers for Cancer are those associated with caring. Thus, nursing or one of its offshoots springs to mind. Any water-related profession will also appeal, particularly if it concerns complementary medicine or therapies. Less obviously, a career in antiques or as a historian could suit you. Why? Because your caring personality will combine with your nostalgic nature in a highly satisfactory way. You could make a great success of running your own business because you excel at anything that involves dealing with other people. Cancer can make quite a lot of money from running garage sales or junk shops. You have an inborn tendency to hoard, and such a venture enables you to clear the decks as well as make some money.

Your Health

You are prone to health problems associated with the chest, the breasts, or the digestive system. Coughs and colds can be severe and difficult to alleviate. Some ailments, such as indigestion, stomach ulcers, and bowel problems can be brought about by stress. Try to avoid worry, which can play havoc with your nervous system.

Cancerian women should examine their breasts regularly in addition to having periodical medical checkups—note the plural. Don't have one checkup and, if you're given the all clear, think that you need never attend the clinic again. There's no need for alarm, but it's better to be safe than sorry.

Most Cancerians are reasonably healthy but, because you are instinctively aware of any bodily imbalances, you may tend to worry about your health. The best remedy for this is a quick visit to the doctor to set your mind at rest.

What You Look for in a Partner

Because you are an extremely sensitive person, you will need an equally sensitive partner—one who can notice your feelings without needing to be told. You want a lover who can tolerate your occasional moodiness and one who will respect your need for personal space. Women of this sign seek a protective partner, and Cancer men look for a strong maternal instinct in their lovers. Most Cancerians can be rather touchy and reluctant to express their feelings, so your partner must be prepared for you to withdraw into your shell for no apparent reason. Face it—you're not easy to live with, but with the right person you can build a loving and long-lasting partnership.

Three Compatible Signs

Capricorn

A partnership with Capricorn is the most likely to result in mutual happiness and success. This sign will offer you companionship and may even succeed in making serious Cancer laugh. The Capricorn's common sense will help to control your own wilder flights of fancy and alleviate your tendency to worry. If you and your partner are not in the first flush of youth, or if there is a big age difference between you, this union should work particularly well. Oddly, many second marriages are Cancer-Capricorn alliances. Cancer is apt to be clinging, but this suits Capricorns well because they prefer to do everything together. Overall, a Cancer-Capricorn pairing could be remarkably successful and long lasting.

Taurus

Taurus is another sign that could provide sensitive Cancer with a happy and durable partnership. You share a dedication to your home and family that will ensure a stable relationship. You both have plenty of common sense and a similar outlook on life. Another advantage here is that Taurus is something of a financial wizard so will avoid the money problems that worry Cancer so much. This couple will make wonderful parents, and, for them, the arrival of a family provides the final addition to their happiness. To outsiders, a Cancer-Taurus partnership may appear humdrum, but to the people concerned it can be blissful.

Pisces

Pisces, like Cancer, is a water sign, and there is likely to be a mystical or spiritual affinity between you. You may even be convinced that you have been together in past lives, and this could mean that you will ignore present life differences concerning age, background, education, and temperament. In this relationship, hurt feelings are unlikely, as you're both extremely sensitive and therefore caring of the other person. Cancer is a little more practical than Pisces on the domestic front, though both value a quiet and comfortable home. You're both extremely loyal and, indeed, are likely to be so wrapped up in your mystical partnership that the thought of infidelity won't even cross your minds. The Cancer-Pisces relationship will be unusual in many ways, but it's likely to be permanent.

Where to Find Your Partner

Capricorn is ambitious and hardworking. Capricorns may be self-employed as shopkeepers, writers, accountants, or farmers. Look for them in schools, too, at parent-teacher meetings. Capricorns make superb head teachers. Because this is an earth sign, their hobbies probably include gardening, so look for them at horticultural events. They're likely, too, to belong to any organization concerning "green" issues or the fate of the planet. One thing is for sure, though—wherever you find your Capricorn, he or she is sure to be a big fish in the pond.

Taurus, on the other hand, is likely to be one of the team. Taureans are not ambitious people, though success is important to them since it represents security and stability. They're clever with money, so you may find them in a bank or as the treasurer of some local organization or club. Many Taureans possess artistic or musical talent. Look for them in art groups or musical societies, and in singing classes, because they often have beautiful voices. They are drawn to the caring professions, so you may find your Taurus in a hospital or even as a vet, because they love animals. They also tend to work in the fields of beauty, gardening, farming, and catering, so look out for them in these areas.

Pisceans have a wide variety of interests and can be successful in a number of careers. They're not materialistic or ambitious and are usually content to work behind the scenes on any project. You'll probably find them by the ocean or maybe reading tarot cards at garden parties, because Pisces has a strong psychic streak. Join a writers' circle or poetry group, and you'll almost certainly find Pisces among the members. Like Taureans, they're passionate about animals and their caring nature leads them into a number of charitable organizations, professional and otherwise.

How to Please Your Lover

Capricorns aren't much given to gallivanting, though they enjoy a visit to a concert or a good restaurant occasionally. They're prudent people who do not appreciate any extravagant or reckless gestures on your part. They'll appreciate good jewelry because it can be regarded as an investment, and insurance against hard times. Choose silver in preference to gold, and turquoise or amethyst stones. They like subdued colors and prefer "quiet" flowers like pansies to more expensive blooms. Overall, the best way to please your Capricorn lover is to provide the stable, ordered, comfortable, and economic lifestyle he or she prefers.

Taurus, too, is a reserved sort of person and prefers the quiet life. On the other hand, Taureans do appreciate anything expensive and of good quality. If you take Taurus out for a meal, ensure that the restaurant is first-class as far as food, service, and surroundings are concerned. Taurus loves delicate jewelry. Choose emeralds in a type of fragile, almost invisible setting.

Pisces loves water. Take Pisceans fishing, swimming, rowing on the river, or on a trip to the ocean. They don't like noise and crowds, so anywhere peaceful and quiet will please them. In spring, suggest a country walk to a beautifully landscaped garden or to a garden center. An early morning trip to a flower market would be the sort of unusual and interesting trip that they enjoy. When it comes to food, they love salads and fruit, and vegetarian restaurants are favored.

Leo

July 23 to August 22

Gender:	*Masculine/Extrovert*
Element:	*Fire*
Quality:	*Fixed*
Ruling Planet:	*The Sun*

On the day that you were born, the Sun was in the fire sign of Leo, the fifth sign of the zodiac. Leo is a fixed sign, indicating strength and stability. Your symbol is the lion, an emblem of strength, authority, and confidence. This is a masculine sign and is ruled by the Sun, the lord of the solar system, which endows you with your regal air.

Leo Characteristics

All Leos will exhibit majestic qualities and will expect others to recognize their superior status. The word *modesty* is not in your vocabulary. You feel that the center of the stage is yours, by right, and anyone who tries to usurp your position will be summarily dealt with. Your need for recognition is your main motivation in all aspects of life. At the same time, you are generous in heart and spirit and like others to enjoy life as much as you do.

It is no coincidence that a group of lions is called a pride. All Leos are intensely proud, but this attitude can sometimes lead to a fall. When this happens, you will slink away, muttering that you are right and everybody else is a fool. This ultraconfident attitude may sometimes be seen by others as bragging and boasting.

An orderly, organized life is essential to you. This need also extends to the lives of other people, where you tend to take over if given the slightest opportunity. Of all the signs, you are most in danger of becoming a power freak. Enthusiastic and creative, you need to fill your days to the brim with action. You can't bear to waste time or talent, whether it's your own or somebody else's.

What You Look Like

Short or tall, most Leos are well proportioned and carry themselves well. You're likely to have thick hair that is fair or red if you belong to a white race, and you probably sweep it back from your forehead, accentuating your leonine appearance. Your eyes, whatever their color, will be large and fearless.

Leos dress to impress and insist on first-rate quality. You'd much prefer to have two expensive outfits than half a dozen cheap ones. True to your standing as king of the jungle, only the best is good enough. Leo favors red, purple, and gold, the opulent colors associated with the Sun and royalty.

Leo in Love

In affairs of the heart, the leonine nature comes to the fore. A Leo woman expects to be wooed by a prince among men. A male Leo wants a beautiful princess whom he can dazzle with his sparkling, charismatic personality. If your partner turns out to be wealthy—well, that's exactly what Leo deserves, isn't it?

A one-sided romance is no good to a Leo. It's essential that you receive as much love as you give. You're a wonderful lover who has the ability to make your partner feel special. Just be sure that your partner realizes that friendship and unconditional love matter to you every bit as much as sex—though you're no slouch in the bedroom.

Leos make absolutely loyal and supportive partners, but you also demand quite a lot in return. You expect to be proud to introduce your lover to other people, and you require them to exhibit the same high standards of behavior and appearance as you do.

You are likely to know your partner for some time before you commit yourself. It is essential for you to have a harmonious home background and you realize that, in order to obtain this, the partners need to know each other well. Love from a stranger is not for Leo.

Your Career

All Leos are showpeople. It's essential that you hold a position of authority where other people will look up to you. If you have acting talent, the theater, films, or television are natural venues for you. Even if you start by sweeping the stage, you'll have your eye on the leading role. You need not act; you can be equally happy as a director, researcher, camera, or a sound recorder. However, you must be in charge. Leos find it almost impossible to take orders.

Whatever work you do, it is essential that you enjoy it. If you don't, you'll soon be out in search of a new venture. Because you are so confident and capable, finding work is not difficult for you. Leo can be markedly successful as a teacher, where you'll find a group of people who will believe every word you say. What could be more satisfying for Leo? You have marked creative talents and you will be happiest and most successful in any position that uses these.

Some Leos do have a lazy streak. This is not immediately obvious, but you may tend to rush about madly for a time only to slump into an uninterested attitude if you are disappointed in any way. Avoid being overbearing, too. This is part of your fixed-sign nature, and you need to be a little more flexible when dealing with other people. In all your relationships, endeavor to prove that your roar is considerably worse than your bite.

Your Health

Because of your constant struggle for supremacy, you may be prone to stress, and this could lead to heart trouble, which is always a danger for Leo. Yours is the sign that rules the heart and the back—so leave the piano for others to move, while you advise on how the job can best be done. You like your food, too, and you sometimes use comfort eating to alleviate stress. Compromise by getting a fair amount of exercise, such as cycling or swimming, and by at least trying to eat sensibly.

Leos hate to be ill and make terrible patients. To you, illness equates with weakness. Try to endure the enforced inactivity with a good grace, and don't return to work until your medical adviser says you may. Why not indulge your lazy streak for once?

What You Look for in a Partner

Because you have such a demanding nature, you're likely to require a great deal (probably too much) from your lover. You will certainly expect your partner to respect and admire you and to tell you so, frequently. Nothing pleases you more than a family gathering, so it's important that your partner share your clannish instincts. Leo doesn't much like change, and you'll appreciate a partner who will be content to remain in the same house for years. You are choosy, so your partner will need to meet your exacting requirements as far as speech, behavior, and appearance are concerned. Leo is loyal and stable in any relationship, and these are the qualities you will demand, above all else, from your companion.

Three Compatible Signs

Libra

A Leo-Libra union should be fine, providing there are no financial problems. Both partners enjoy the good things in life and like to create an impression of culture and affluence. You both enjoy what can be termed *gracious living* and are prepared to work hard to achieve this lifestyle. Libra is an essentially feminine sign and needs a steady supply of TLC—something that Leo is well equipped to give. In return, Libra must provide the appreciation and consideration Leo requires. Any arguments that do arise can be settled by Libra's well-balanced attitude and Leo's generous nature. A Leo-Libra partnership should be harmonious and long-lasting.

Scorpio
Scorpio may seem an unlikely partner for Leo, but this pairing can often work remarkably well. Because both Scorpio and Leo are strong characters and both are fixed signs, this will not be a peaceful relationship. The main point of conflict is likely to be money. Leo is not cheap but likes to spend wisely. Scorpio is given to sudden bouts of extravagance that are likely to provoke leonine roars of disapproval. The best solution to this problem is to have separate bank accounts. To some extent, this partnership can be regarded as the attraction of opposites. However, given your shared capacity for love and loyalty, a Leo-Scorpio relationship can be extremely successful—and never boring.

Virgo
An alliance between Leo and Virgo is one that often puzzles other people because they seem such an unlikely couple. Yet they have a number of complementary attributes that can increase the union's chances of success. Virgo, the perfectionist, will provide the comfortable and beautiful home all Leos demand. Leo loves doing things in a big way, and Virgo will supply the organization needed to support these aspirations. Both partners have a great deal of pride. They quickly reach an agreement about what each of them expects from the partnership, and both possess the stability to achieve their aims. This may all sound cold, calculated, and dull, but a Leo-Virgo relationship is certainly not lacking in passion and can be immensely satisfying to both partners.

Where to Find Your Partner
Libra prefers teamwork to lone ventures, so you will probably find your partner in the sort of job where there are plenty of people around. Librans dislike noise and bustle, though, and prefer the calm elegance of a legal office, a library, or something similar.

Social or welfare work may appeal, as Librans' balanced outlook helps them to sort out all types of complex problems. They love music, so you'll find them at concerts or taking active part in a band or at a small club devoted to whatever pop music is on the cutting edge at the time. Discussion groups appeal to them. Other hobbies may include cooking, art classes, and computer clubs.

Scorpios are great achievers, so you will find them in any situation that requires ambition. They also love to investigate and analyze problems and often work as pathologists, market analysts, researchers, detectives, or police officers. You may find them in psychic societies, thanks to their urge to investigate. These people are athletic and energetic. You'll find them at soccer games and boxing matches or sometimes as race-car drivers. They're interested in archeology, psychology, and any scientific hobby that requires painstaking attention.

Virgo is critical, intelligent, and practical. You'll find your Virgo partner in jobs where extremely detailed work is needed. Virgos need to serve, so may well be found as teachers, psychologists, or counselors. As far as leisure activities are concerned, they enjoy the theater, movies, and music—though they'll invariably be critical of any performance. For some reason, weaving is a popular hobby with Virgos, and they have the patience to produce beautiful work. They certainly won't be satisfied with less.

How to Please Your Lover

Libra likes an orderly life, so don't expect your partner to do things impulsively. Librans will enjoy a gourmet meal at a quiet (and expensive) restaurant or a visit to the opera, but everything must be planned. Pushing through noisy crowds or rushing to catch a train will destroy their enjoyment of the occasion.

Scorpios are not easy to please and, whatever you offer, they will expect the gift to be beautifully packaged. They like unusual (and costly looking) gifts that they can nonchalantly display to friends, and if you assure them that you've hunted high and low for weeks to find that one perfect item, they will positively purr with pleasure.

Virgo is always delighted to be given books, preferably beautifully bound hardbacks, but do ensure that your choice is not already included in their library. Perhaps a gift certificate to a bookstore, though admittedly an uninspiring gift, would be a better choice. Virgos don't really enjoy personal presents like clothing or toiletries, but will greatly appreciate tickets for a show or a visit to a garden center—in fact, anything to do with their hobbies and leisure interests.

Virgo

August 23 to September 22

Gender: *Feminine/Introvert*
Element: *Earth*
Quality: *Mutable*
Ruling Planet: *Mercury*

On the day that you were born, the Sun was in the earth sign of Virgo, the sixth sign of the zodiac. Virgo is a mutable sign, indicating that you are always open to change and highly adaptable. Your symbol is the virgin, who is shown holding a sheaf of wheat. This represents the fruitfulness of the earth and, by association, the fertile female. As you would expect, Virgo is a feminine sign, ruled by Mercury, the messenger of the gods.

Virgo Characteristics

The wheat sheaf that the Virgin carries represents your Earth Mother or nurturing tendencies. Virgos tend to be idealistic and are often diffident, as befits a virgin. However, you can be lively and talkative, particularly when you are with family or friends. You do tend to seem reserved, but those who know you well will be aware that you have a kind heart and will do anything for anybody.

Virgo is apt to be fussy and hypercritical, with a keen eye for detail. This critical tendency is often most marked where you yourself are concerned. You have extremely high standards and seldom trust other people to meet them, so that you try to do everything yourself. Then, if you fail in your endeavors, you may become bitter and cynical. You possess a lot of nervous energy and need to be constantly occupied if you are to avoid the worrying tendency so marked in your nature.

Practicality is one of your virtues. You like to analyze everything so that you can come up with a logical working plan for any situation. Intellectually, you're very bright, and learning comes easily to you.

What You Look Like

Virgos are innately fastidious and go to great lengths to be constantly clean and immaculate. Your hair, usually thick, is impeccably groomed, and your eyes have a gentle, caring expression. Whether or not you are strictly handsome, you will project an aura of dignity and self-assurance. Whatever your age, your youthful appearance is the envy of your peers.

Clothes are important to you and you tend to spend a lot of money on them. Your tastes are conservative and you dress mainly in somber colors, such as gray and dark blue. No matter what color your clothing, it is sure to be well tailored and correct for the occasion.

Virgo in Love

You will be a trustworthy partner, generous to a fault with the one you love, but not until you have formed a lasting relationship. You need to be 110 percent sure that this is the real thing before committing yourself to any partnership, and this can take a long time. It's not your bashfulness that holds you back, but your faultfinding perfectionism that inhibits you.

You will be instantly and constantly aware of any minor flaw in your potential partner and, if he or she fails to measure up to your requirements, you'll drop that individual immediately. Then you will feel guilty, thus exacerbating your lack of self-esteem.

When you do finally make up your mind and embark on a permanent relationship, you are completely faithful and kind.

Being an earth sign, you are a surprisingly adept lover. Should you discover that you've made a mistake, your kindness and sense of duty, not to mention your dislike of emotional upheaval, will probably mean that you'll stay put and try again.

Your Career

No Virgo was ever afraid of work. Indeed, the term *workaholic* could have been invented for people born under this sign. The typical Virgo is compulsively analytical and has a shrewd business sense and a keen eye for to detail. This means that you will be an expert in your chosen line of work, and most likely the one selected for promotion. To you, time is money, and money is time, and you hate to waste either.

With your link to Mercury, you love the written word in any form. In fact, many writers are Virgos. You seldom seek the spotlight, preferring to work conscientiously behind the scenes, though you do expect your talents to be recognized. This should be seen as strength, rather than a weakness. Careful types like you are just as valuable as the hot-blooded firebrands of this world. You are ideally suited to any career that requires meticulous detailed analysis. Job security is important to you, and you like a post in which you have a clearly spelled-out agenda. You dislike taking the initiative for fear of making a mistake and appearing incompetent. This means that you make an efficient and trustworthy personal assistant. As mentioned earlier, many writers are Virgos. Even if a career as an author doesn't appeal to you, there are other openings—for instance, in publishing, in which your flair for words will be useful.

Your Health

Virgos are natural-born worriers, and any part of the body that shows the slightest deviation from normal can be a source of anxiety. Of all the signs in the zodiac, Virgo is the most prone to hypochondria. This may cause problems with your nervous system, resulting in migraines and similar ailments. Worrying may also cause you to be a heavy smoker, and we don't need to go into any detail about the problems that habit may create.

When you feel hungry, you tend to eat anything at hand. This could upset your digestive system and lead to a number of ailments. Virgo often suffers from skin problems. You are prone to eczema, psoriasis, and sunburn.

What You Look for in a Partner

You're likely to have high expectations of your partner in many ways. You'll certainly demand an intellect to match your own, and similar all-encompassing high standards. Strangely, for such a fastidious sign, you tend to be untidy—so you'll need a lover who will put up with this and who will clear up after you.

Money is important to you, and you'll expect the household budget to be carefully worked out. Your perfectionist trait appears here because you want the best of everything in food and surroundings. It follows, therefore, that your partner must be something of an economist.

Above all, you need a partner who will understand your Virgo ways and have a marked degree of tolerance, particularly insofar as your streak of laziness is concerned.

Three Compatible Signs

Cancer

Cancer, like Virgo, is often hesitant about embarking on any serious relationship, but once the commitment is made, Cancer gives, and expects, total reliability. You will also have in common a shrewd business sense and a willingness to work hard to achieve your aims. Both of you are family-minded and share a compassionate attitude toward those less fortunate than yourselves. Cancer also possesses most of the domestic virtues Virgo expects in a partner.

Difficulties may arise concerning Cancer's moodiness and Virgo's tendency to criticize. Most of these problems can be solved by sensible discussion, providing you are both willing to express your feelings without hostility. You are well matched intellectually and you can develop joint interests to provide a firm foundation to your partnership. Since you both have a strong sense of duty, a Virgo-Cancer alliance can be quietly but enduringly satisfactory.

Gemini

Gemini and Virgo are both ruled by Mercury, the planet of communication, so you shouldn't have any awkward silences. However, it takes more than conversation to make a partnership successful. Serious Virgo may be alternately enchanted and infuriated by Gemini's flighty escapades, while Gemini may often be bored by your pedantic approach. You share a love of words and learning, and Gemini will go more than halfway to meet Virgo's needs. Geminis are not domesticated but willingly pay for somebody else to run the household and are always happy to entertain family and friends. You're both very much aware of the value of money. Both Gemini and Virgo are innately fastidious about the way they look. You also share a tendency to worry. However, if you're each prepared to allow your partner some needed space and if you can curb your sarcastic tongue, the Virgo-Gemini pairing could be a good match.

Pisces

Pisces is the sign opposite Virgo, so you complement each other well. You both have compassionate, caring natures, though Pisces is more likely than Virgo to put emotions into words. Stable Virgo will enjoy feeling protective toward vulnerable Pisces. Indeed, since there is always something of the child in the Pisces makeup, this pairing could result in you feeling almost parental toward your partner at times. You are both easily depressed, but as long as this doesn't happen simultaneously, it need not be a problem. Pisces is intensely loving and will do almost anything to please a partner, but Pisceans are ultrasensitive and easily hurt. If you can cope with their mood swings and they can tolerate your critical attitude, a Virgo-Pisces alliance could be extremely happy.

Where to Find Your Partner

Cancerians often work in the catering industry, so you'll find them in hotels, restaurants, hospitals, or even in cooking classes—as either teacher or pupil. They like water, too, so regattas or boat shows could interest them, and you're almost sure to find them at a swimming pool or sailing club. Because their families mean a lot to them, they may be members of genealogical societies, and because they're great collectors, they'll visit auctions and garage sales.

Geminis have a multitude of interests, often flitting between one enthusiasm and another. However, any form of communication is important to them, so they'll probably work in public relations, on a local newspaper, as a telephone salesperson, or in a political party. They're not into contact sports, but table tennis, archery, or pool may appeal. You'll almost certainly find Gemini in amateur dramatic societies, where they'll probably play the leading role, or at dancing classes.

Pisceans are intuitive, impressionable, and sympathetic. Their need to be of service leads them to work as doctors or nurses, counselors, or even in the church. They are extremely artistic, so are often members of writing groups, poetry circles, art classes, or musical societies. Pisces loves anything that has an element of fantasy or mystery about it and has strong psychic leanings.

How to Please Your Lover

Cancer is fascinated by the past, so a trip to a museum or antiques fair cannot fail to please. If you're hardup, a tour of the local junk shops will probably be appreciated. As mentioned previously, Cancerians are great collectors. Find out what most interests them and try to add to their collection from time to time. Frequent small gifts will be much more appreciated than one large item. They love cooking, so kitchen equipment is sure to please. If you're looking for jewelry, try to find antique pearls.

Geminis have a generous nature, and love to receive gifts. Though they'll be delighted with almost anything, simply because it is a gift, they particularly love flowers, especially lily of the valley or lavender. They are avid readers, so the latest bestseller will be well received, particularly if it is attractively wrapped. In fact, Gemini is easily pleased, but if you can produce a gift that is not only unusual but also extremely fashionable, you're going to score well.

Pisces loves jewelry, preferably amethysts or moonstones in a fragile setting, and perfume—but nothing too heavy or sophisticated. The current vogue for flower scents is very much to Pisceans' taste, and they will be grateful for toiletries made from natural ingredients. Gifts for the home, such as Tiffany lamps or cut-glass dishes, will also be treasured.

Libra

September 23 to October 22

Gender: *Masculine/Extrovert*
Element: *Air*
Quality: *Cardinal*
Ruling Planet: *Venus*

On the day that you were born, the Sun was in the air sign of Libra, the seventh sign of the zodiac. This is a cardinal sign, producing people who are quick-witted and courageous. The symbol for Libra is the scales, signifying your well-balanced ability to see both sides of any issue. Libra is a masculine sign, ruled by Venus, the planet of love.

Libra Characteristics

Librans' major attribute is their need to achieve balance and harmony in every aspect of their lives—and often in other people's. Sometimes you're rather slow in reaching a decision, because you explore all options before making up your mind. This habit may irritate some people but, in your favor, it must be said that once you've decided on anything, you stick with it.

Despite the trait mentioned above, you're a doer rather than a thinker. Even so, no matter how strongly you feel, you use your intelligence before springing into action. You also have clearly defined opinions about most things and don't hesitate to express them. Fair play is important to you, and you have instinctive sympathy for the underdog.

You dislike taking orders, but your innate desire to perform well ensures that you're trustworthy and a hard worker. Be on your guard not to sound petulant if you have to accept instructions from another person. This is a side of your nature that can let you down occasionally.

What You Look Like

Librans are usually pleasant-looking people, and if you're lucky, you will almost certainly have a dimple in your cheeks or chin. Your smile can charm the birds from the trees and reveals even, well-cared-for teeth, possibly with a gap between the front two. Your eyes are likely to be large, with a steady gaze. Most Librans have a clear, well-modulated voice.

Clothes are important to you, and you always strive to match your appearance to the occasion. You have quiet good taste, with a preference for subtle colors and simple styles. Above all, everything you wear is immaculately clean and perfectly ironed. It is said that you can spot a Libra by their shoes—always in good condition and positively gleaming.

Libra in Love

If you're looking for a partner, be careful. You above all others are a sucker for flattery. You thrive on admiration and you'll fall head-over-heels in love—for the time being, anyway. Then you'll fall just as quickly for the next sycophant who comes along. Why do you do this? The answer is simple. Libra is happy only when in the company of other people. You are terrified of being alone, so all relationships are of primary importance to you.

Eventually, you are sure to realize that you need to find someone with whom you can have a completely harmonious relationship. This won't happen until you meet the one person who can sit on the other side of the scales and balance you in all respects. Without this, your relationship will have a highly uncertain future. You hate arguments, and anyone who rocks the boat—or tips the scales—will get short shrift from you.

Finding your partner may not be as difficult as it sounds, since you do seem attract the right sort of person. Once this person appears, you'll think that all your birthdays have come at once. Just ensure that your lover remembers how much you need reassurance and appreciation for every little loving gesture.

Your Career

For you, an occupation that includes human relationships is essential. With your innate sense of justice, tact, and diplomacy, you make a splendid counselor or arbitrator. Marriage counseling or work in a trade union will come naturally to you. You can succeed in any aspect of law, diplomacy, or politics.

Your balanced outlook promises success in the design areas of fashion, interior decorating, and graphics. Art appeals strongly to you and you could make a successful dealer. Your fluent speech and charming manner could lead to a successful career in any form of sales.

In short, you are capable of succeeding in many different fields, but don't hesitate for too long about which one to tackle. As long as you work in a quiet and harmonious environment away from noise and dirt, your success should be assured.

Your Health

Because balance is so important to you, your mantra should be moderation in all things. Libra rules the lower back, kidneys, and ovaries, giving you a tendency to such ailments as lumbago. Try to lead a healthy lifestyle and eat a simple diet. Drink as much water as you can; it is quite literally the elixir of life to you.

The problem here is that you are such a conscientious worker and that you love parties—your own or other people's. As a result, you may find yourself out of sorts at frequent intervals. Redress the balance with plenty of physical exercise and fresh air, and increase your intake of water.

Your general well-being will improve all around if you ensure that you regularly get a good night's sleep. A sleep debt is not something that a Libran can afford to carry, so at least try to get to bed early two or three times a week.

What You Look for in a Partner

Because Libra hates to be alone, you need a great deal of attention and companionship from your partner. Anyone who travels a lot on business or does shift work is unlikely to suit you. Ideally, your lover will be home before you in the evenings and still there when you leave for work in the morning.

You'll enjoy having a partner who is able to help you make decisions. You wouldn't get along well with a bossy person but will appreciate somebody who can weigh up the pros and cons of a situation and help you to make up your mind.

A partner who enjoys loud music, flamboyant behavior, and gaudy clothes won't suit you, but you're unlikely to be attracted to this sort of person, anyway. It's essential for you to have a lover who shares your own quiet and cultured tastes. In fact, Libran partnerships can often be described as a marriage of the minds, though these people can be surprisingly sexy and romantic.

Three Compatible Signs

Gemini

Gemini, like you, is pleasant and easygoing, and this could almost be a case of love at first sight. However, no matter how strongly cautious Libra is attracted to the bubbly Gemini personality, you will take your time to consider the situation carefully. Gemini isn't very good at reaching decisions, either, so the two of you could drift along in a romantic haze for a considerable time before deciding to make a firm commitment. You must be prepared to tolerate Gemini's sharp tongue, and Gemini must be able to cope with your moods, but you're both good-tempered so this shouldn't be too much of a problem. Your shared interest in music and the arts and the good things of life will undoubtedly form a strong bond between you. There won't be many fireworks here, but a Libra-Gemini pairing should be stable and harmonious.

Leo

Leo is invariably the type of mate who demands a lot from his or her partner; fortunately, Libra is well able to measure up to these requirements. You both enjoy material comforts and, if this relationship is to work, you need to sort out any financial problems early on. This should not be difficult, given Leo's generous streak and your ardent desire for a well-balanced life—and bank account. Leo is family-oriented and very given to gatherings of the clan. Since Libra hates being alone, you'll be happy to go along with this. You may each need to make a few adjustments about living together, but there's a lot going for a Libra-Leo pairing and, given commitment on both sides, this should be a successful partnership.

Aquarius

Aquarius and Libra fit together like two pieces in a jigsaw puzzle. This may sound as if you're joined at the hip, but that's not so. You both enjoy your own space but also need to feel that there is one special person available to help you when needed. Aquarius needs to remember that Libra likes plenty of praise and demonstrative affection. You share a love of company and are both socially adept, so that you're likely to be one of the most popular couples in your group. The weakest point here is that Aquarius is apt to be forgetful about communicating and Libra hates to feel ignored. Keep the communication flowing smoothly and the Libra-Aquarius partnership should be a resounding success.

Where to Find Your Partner

Geminis adore talking, so they can be found in any job that relates to communication. They prefer to talk face to face or on the phone, but they also work in any job that requires frequent e-mailing and keeping in frequent contact with others. The cheerful Gemini is the one with a collection of e-mailed jokes downloaded onto his or her desktop! Geminis enjoy travel, so you may meet up with them when you are on vacation. They're clever with their hands, too, so you may find them at some event to do with crafts or gadgets.

These people love to communicate, so you can find them working as teachers or telephone operators, in sales and customer service posts, and in the media. Some are drawn to the worlds of construction and garden design. Otherwise, try a sports club, an astrology group, or a Masonic or similar social organization such as the social or fund-raising side of a church, mosque, or temple.

Leo is health-conscious, so will almost certainly have a fitness routine. This means you may meet at the gym, at a swimming pool, or when you're out jogging. Leos like movement and usually excel at sports like tennis, running, and diving. They'll enjoy playing games at their frequent family parties and are often keen members of theater clubs or amateur dramatic societies.

Aquarius can be found in any occupation or pastime that involves a group of people. Aquarians can be dancers, scientists, charity workers, or can work in any job that requires forward thinking and experimentation. Aquarian leisure interests are equally varied. They include community work, local politics, flying, music, and dancing—and they'll be particularly happy if they're the star of the show in whatever they undertake.

How to Please Your Lover

Gemini loves small gifts, but this is not necessarily an inexpensive option, particularly if you're offering jewelry, where they have a taste for sapphires and jade. Don't make the mistake of asking your Gemini partner to choose his or her own gifts, as Geminis adore surprises. Even if it's not exactly what they were hoping for, they'll be delighted that you've gone to the trouble of choosing something particularly for them, and wrapping it beautifully.

Leo, on the other hand, thinks that big is beautiful. Leos look for unusual and impressive presents, so on no account should you admit that you picked up the gift on sale at the mall. Leos particularly love the rich royal red of rubies, and even the males will happily wear jewelry, providing it is in good taste. Leos love to feel that everything they have is exclusive and expensive. Do your best to foster this impression and your partner will be eternally grateful.

Aquarians are fussy about what they consider acceptable gifts. Above all, anything you give your partner must be genuine rather than fake, unless the object is funky or hard to obtain. They'll enjoy new published books, magazine subscriptions, or theater tickets. However, if you really want to score with your Aquarius lover you'll choose the latest piece of electronic or communications equipment.

Scorpio

October 23 to November 21

Gender:	*Feminine/Introvert*
Element:	*Water*
Quality:	*Fixed*
Ruling Planet:	*Mars/Pluto*

On the day that you were born, the Sun was in the water sign of Scorpio, the eighth sign of the zodiac. This is a fixed sign, showing that you will be strong and unyielding in everything you undertake. The symbol for Scorpio is a scorpion, one of nature's survivors. However, you also have a second symbol, the eagle, soaring overhead, way above life's problems, unseen, but missing nothing. Both symbols say a lot about the typical Scorpio nature. Scorpio also has two ruling planets—Mars, the god of war, and Pluto, the god of the underworld and of regeneration.

Scorpio Characteristics

You never do anything halfway and are notorious for rejecting any form of opposition to your plans. Anyone who upsets you or a member of your family, or even one of your pets (intentionally or otherwise), could be in trouble.

Scorpio is unpredictable, passionate, and intense. You will never accept anything at face value. Finding out what makes people tick is your favorite pastime, because you keep on digging and delving until you find out everything you want to know. You may then use that knowledge to your own advantage. To a Scorpio, knowledge is power—and power means that you can be in control. If you lose that control, the sting in your tail provides a formidable weapon. Most Scorpios are indifferent to what other people own or their achievements, and they can't be bothered to keep up with the Joneses. The reason for this is that Scorpio's intense self-interest means that this sign focuses mainly on its own achievements and possessions. It is the Joneses who struggle to keep up with Scorpio! You don't hesitate to punish an injury but neither do you forget a kindness.

Dignity is important to you, and you strive to maintain it in all circumstances. Your home and family are the mainstays of your life. Friends may be few in number, but you are very loyal to those you do have.

What You Look Like

Your most distinctive feature is undoubtedly your eyes, which are deep-set and penetrating with an almost hypnotic quality. You're likely to have strong features and thick eyebrows, which can give you a frowning expression. When you're studying somebody else, as you often do, you tend to incline your head and look up from beneath your brows, which is a habit that some people find disconcerting. You probably have thick hair and take great pride in it.

You're large-boned and heavier than you would like, but your body will almost certainly be well proportioned. Your taste in clothes will be for apparel that enhances your dignified appearance, and you'll feel most comfortable in deep shades of red or black.

Scorpio in Love

Yours is the most passionate sign of the zodiac, and those who fall in love with you soon find out how deeply amorous you can be. Let's not beat around the bush. Scorpio rules the reproductive organs, and beneath that smoldering exterior lays a lot of raw sexual energy. Your emotions run deep but you can hold them in check. You are capable of tremendous self-control but, when you see the green light, you don't hold back—it's all systems go with you. However, true to your nature, even during these most intimate moments, you like to be the dominant partner.

Scorpios can put on public displays of temper or emotion, because they love to be the center of attention. When you meet your life partner, you will be intensely possessive and there will be fireworks if you imagine that they are even glancing at anyone else. Though you are reluctant to admit it, you are extremely dependent on your partner. In private, you will display the utmost tenderness.

Sex is extremely important to you, and any problems in this side of your relationship will upset and infuriate you. Whatever the difficulty, you will see it as a personal failure, yet be too embarrassed to seek help or even to discuss the situation with your partner.

Your Career

Being under the influence of Pluto makes you want to delve into the deepest mysteries of life. Make use of this talent in finding your occupation. Research and investigation offer many opportunities for you. Any form of detective work seems to have been made for Scorpios. You have a unique ability to dig out the truth from given facts, and have an instinctive understanding of body language.

Your Health

Your main areas of weakness are the lower spine and the digestion. Therefore, slipped discs, sciatica, lumbago, or any other back pain are recurring problems. Your stomach is sensitive, too, so you may suffer from indigestion, a hiatal hernia or the kind of esophagus that narrows, so that food gets stuck on its way down. You like spicy food, but it may not like you!

The reproductive organs can be problematic, and Scorpio women may have problems relating to conception or childbirth. It is interesting to note that many Scorpios don't have children at all, not because they can't but because they prefer pets and animals to children. The main thing is to take any symptoms seriously and not to hesitate until they become a real problem.

What You Look for in a Partner

In line with the aloof and dignified air you present to the public, you need a partner in whom you can take pride and who will never embarrass you. You're not really concerned about whether or not that person is good-looking, but they must be intelligent, socially at ease, and presentable. It helps if your partner has a successful career or absorbing leisure interests, and you will do everything possible to support them.

You can't tolerate a chatterbox, and neither will you enjoy life with somebody who wants to go out all the time. The institution of marriage is important to you and you need a partner who will share your high ideals, so that you can build a beautiful home and a satisfying life together.

Thanks to your strong sex drive, you must have a partner who is equally amorous but very faithful. Your partner also needs to understand that your secretive Scorpio nature means that you are extremely unlikely to kiss and tell, no matter what the subject. Your arrogance and conviction that you are always right can cause problems, and you're unlikely to discuss them or even have a good argument in an attempt to reach a compromise. Indeed, that word is almost missing from your vocabulary.

Three Compatible Signs

Leo

The initial attraction between Leo and Scorpio is overwhelming, but what happens after that is in the hands of the gods—or the two people concerned. You're both highly sexed and passionate but, where Leos will express their feelings, Scorpio is apt to be secretive. Indeed, your apparent coldness could even result in Leo playing away from home at times. The differences in your attitudes, particularly regarding money, can result in some violent storms. If you can control (or conceal?) your bouts of extravagance and be a little more demonstrative, the Scorpio-Leo relationship could be exciting and highly rewarding.

Cancer

Cancer, with those dangerous claws, and Scorpio, with that deadly sting in the tail, have much in common. However, the claws and the stinger will not be noticeable in this relationship. Both are very loyal and have a strong sense of duty. You will delight in the opportunity to show the latent tenderness in your makeup, strictly in private, of course, and Cancer will revel in the knowledge that you care. Cancer is highly sensitive to your unspoken need for support and will always be there when you're feeling vulnerable. Repay this consideration by allowing your partner to dominate you occasionally. The Scorpio-Cancer alliance is likely to be stable and harmonious, providing you both remember not to give your lover cause for jealousy.

Taurus

Providing Taurus is your intellectual equal, this could be a highly successful partnership. However, you're both very stubborn, and this could create some problems when differences of opinion arise. In particular, Taurus likes to know what's going on—and Scorpio has a decidedly secretive streak. You're both highly sexed, but you should remember that Taurus needs verbal and demonstrative assurance of your devotion. The family home is important to both of you and you make excellent parents. The Scorpio-Taurus partnership is companionable, stable, occasionally romantic, and usually long-lasting.

Where to Find Your Partner

It's easy to identify Leos, because they always stand out from the crowd. They're almost certain to be the leader of any group, and they will occupy a responsible position in business. If a friend invites you along to a family party, don't make an excuse not to attend—this is exactly the sort of function at which you'll find a

Leo, usually organizing everything and everybody. If a game of cards is suggested, Leo will be enthusiastic—Leos are great gamblers.

Cancer loves water. It follows, therefore, that wherever you find water, you will stand a good chance of meeting your Cancer partner. They may work in seaside hotels or restaurants, belong to swimming or boating clubs, and probably enjoy fishing. Cancerians love anything to do with property, so look for then in real estate agencies, time-share outlets, and shops or other organizations that supply goods for the home.

Taurus is musical, so will be found at concerts, in amateur operatic societies, and in musical groups. Because Taureans have an instinctive grasp of financial affairs, you'll find them in any institutions dealing with money, or as the treasurer of a local society. They're clever with creative projects, so they'll gravitate toward craft shops, art groups, and dressmaking classes.

How to Please Your Lover

Leo particularly enjoys receiving large-scale presents, elaborately wrapped. This childlike enthusiasm for unwrapping gifts lasts throughout Leos' lives, so why not use the old surprise method of packing a small gift in the middle of several boxes and layers of paper. Your Leo lover will be more and more excited as each container is removed, and this builds up to positive delight when the gift is finally revealed. If that gift, though small, is also expensive, your Leo lover will be overwhelmed.

Cancer, the financial genius, will automatically assess the price of any gift you offer. Cancerians are not concerned about the value, but if they suspect you paid more than necessary for the object, they'll be uneasy. Their tastes are simple and they appreciate anything of good quality, particularly for the home. Strangely, they also adore luxurious gifts—though if you give them jewelry or perfume they'll probably save it for special days and holidays.

Taurus practicality comes to the fore as far as presents are concerned. At Christmas, for example, a food hamper, a case of wine, or a bottle of exotic liqueur will be gratefully accepted. Buy some good china or glass and add to the set on gift-giving occasions. Taureans like leather, so if you can give your partner hand-made Italian shoes, a Gucci handbag, or elegant luggage, you'll score well. Top tip from a luxury-lover who has little money to spare: look around the thrift, recycled, or secondhand shops in smart areas, and you will find brand name goods there at discount prices.

Sagittarius

November 23 to December 21

Gender: *Masculine/Extrovert*
Element: *Fire*
Quality: *Mutable*
Ruling Planet: *Jupiter*

On the day that you were born, the Sun was in Sagittarius, the ninth sign of the zodiac. This is a masculine fire sign, ruled by the planet Jupiter, the lord of the gods. Sagittarius is a mutable sign, indicating that you are flexible and cooperative, and it is a fire sign, making you positive and plain-spoken. Your symbol is the archer, half-horse and half-human—and therefore sometimes referred to as the centaur.

Sagittarius Characteristics

You are a firebrand, full of enthusiastic energy. Because you are a mutable sign, you are able to adapt to almost any situation. You also love to be free of all restraints and have fun.

You love traveling—the farther the better. Your favorite destinations are those that you hope will enable you to fulfill some idealistic aspiration. The world is your oyster, and your tutor. You learn more from life than you ever will from books. The downside to this trait is that you tend to be restless, always wanting to move on.

Allowing your tongue to get ahead of your brain can be a problem. You are quick to voice your opinion and can be extremely tactless. Take time to listen, consider the facts, and reason things out before you make rash statements. Sagittarius can be incredibly charming, but you lack consistency, and this could lead others to regard you as something of a con artist.

Jupiter is the planet of good fortune, and you often find that you're in the right place at the right time when an opportunity comes along. Not surprisingly, you detest boredom and will go to great lengths to avoid it.

What You Look Like

Sagittarius is usually strong, active, and taller than average. You are likely to have a handsome-smiling face, a long chin, and intelligent, twinkling eyes. Alternatively, you may be small and plump.

You probably have long, thick hair, which in white races is often blond or fair with reddish tints. It tends to fall over your forehead so that you toss your head (like a horse) to throw it back. Although your hair may have a tendency to thin as the years go by, you will retain your youthful appearance and remain physically active well into old age.

You're certainly not a fashion plate, but you have good taste and look after your clothes. All shades of blue, maroon, and purple suit you. Your confident bearing and pleasant manner ensure that you attract attention wherever you go.

Sagittarius in Love

You are lucky in love, and being attractive, you will undoubtedly be able to pick and choose when it comes to finding a partner. The main problem may be your need for complete freedom. Once you have met the right person, you are completely loyal but you still need your own space, and partners may find this difficult to understand.

You're highly sexed and inclined to rush in where angels fear to tread. As soon as your ideal partner lights your fire, you'll want to shower them with gifts before whisking them off to some big adventure in a new and exciting location. However, it is as well to ensure that your partner actually wants this. Don't take too much for granted or get carried away by your enthusiasm.

Although your loyalty to your partner is beyond question, he or she may complain that you are more concerned with universal love than with personal devotion. No matter how deeply you feel about humankind in general, you should first offer a great deal of TLC to your partner.

Your Career

Look for a career that fits in with your appetite for freedom. Working on any sort of production line or sitting behind a desk all day will never satisfy you. Any profession that keeps you on the move will be ideal. If it can also satisfy your intellectual leanings, you should do well.

You're extremely versatile and happily cope with doing several things at once or even with two jobs. Work as a courier or as a sales representative would satisfy your need for travel and variety. You love animals and the open air, so you would probably make a splendid forest ranger.

Sagittarius can be a superb teacher, lawyer, or writer, and may be found in government service. In fact, your versatility prepares you for a wide variety of professions. Just be sure that your love of freedom doesn't lead to frequent job changes—they don't look good on a resume.

Your Health

Sagittarius is the archer, so you are unlikely to experience problems with your arms or shoulders. You'll find that your hips and legs are the regions of your body that most need attention. Replacement hip and knee joints are not uncommon with Sagittarius. As you get older, you may notice increased weight on your hips, thighs, and buttocks because of your tendency to overeat. Blame jovial Jupiter for this weakness and for your tendency to drink too much. For

Sagittarius, social drinking can be a dangerous pastime. You need to treat your liver kindly if you are to avoid problems.

You're fairly strong and healthy. In any case, you have little patience with illness and tend to work through it if you possibly can. Your love of sports may make you accident-prone. Be patient if you suffer from strained muscles or anything similar. If you insist on ignoring such problems, they could give rise to permanent handicaps.

You hate routine of any kind and particularly that associated with sickness. However, your positive attitude helps you to deal quickly with any illnesses that come your way.

What You Look for in a Partner

Above all else, Sagittarius needs freedom. That being so, a possessive or clinging partner is not for you. You need love—the kind that gives encouragement and support, yet at the same time acknowledges your right to your own space and privacy. Your ideal partner will need a good deal of patience to cope with your restlessness and will be happy to accompany you on sudden trips here-there-and everywhere. You need a partner who will be socially at ease in any company.

You're apt to take risks of all kinds, and finance is not your strong point. It will be helpful, therefore, if your partner is money-wise. This may help to counteract your own love of gambling and may even help you with your speculations in stocks and shares. It will be an added advantage if your partner also enjoys sports and the open air.

Three Compatible Signs

Virgo

Virgo and Sagittarius are widely different in many ways, but there is a strong attraction between you. You do share a sense of humor and this could well be the redeeming feature. You may find a Virgo partner somewhat house-proud and persnickety, but, at the same time, you will appreciate the well-ordered and comfortable home

Virgos create. Virgo is more reserved than Sagittarius, and this could work well, allowing you to take center stage when you attend social events together. You're well matched intellectually, but you may be irritated by your partner's habit of worrying. Virgo will certainly not take kindly to your taste for gambling and speculation but is unlikely to complain unless you jeopardize the family savings or the home. Even then, you will find that your partner can be outspoken but never cruel. A Sagittarius-Virgo relationship can be highly successful, providing you both retain your sense of humor.

Capricorn

On the face of it, Capricorn and Sagittarius appear to have little in common, yet sometimes this can be a case of love at first sight. Whether or not the relationship lasts depends largely on other influences in the charts of the two people concerned. Capricorn is easily embarrassed and may find social events difficult to handle. However, you are well able to provide the support your partner needs on such occasions, and once Capricorn feels more at ease, he or she can be charming. You'll enjoy the Capricorn's dry sense of humor, too, and may even be surprised to find your Capricorn partner flirting gently. One of Capricorn's less attractive habits is penny-pinching, and this could lead to arguments about your own behavior where money is concerned. A Sagittarius-Capricorn pairing has a lot going for it but needs a fair amount of tolerance on both sides.

Pisces

Pisces shares your need for freedom and enjoys travel as much as you do. Your mutual love of children augurs well for family life. Many Pisceans are very sociable and enjoy entertaining at home or having a meal out. They usually have a number of friends who are welcome to visit at any time. However, they do enjoy their own company occasionally and will fully understand your own need for space. Life with Pisceans is never dull. They can make a drama out of a late mail delivery or a lost handkerchief. Try not to get impatient with their foibles. They are easily hurt and may then become self-pitying and moody, but a Sagittarius-Pisces partnership can be lasting and immensely rewarding.

Where to Find Your Partner

Virgos are the do-gooders of the zodiac, and this is not meant in any derogatory way. You will find your Virgo partner in any situation where he or she can be of service. Virgos prefer to be part of a team rather than being in charge, and they do like to feel that their efforts are appreciated. Because they can cope with details and analytical work, they excel as accountants or in computing, secretarial work, and publishing. Look for your Virgo partner in dramatic societies or at writing groups. They enjoy spectator sports, or you may meet them at cooking classes.

Capricorn is a workaholic and, whatever their position in a company, they will be efficient, conscientious, and ambitious. You may find your Capricorn lover successfully running his or her own business or in a position of authority in publishing, banking, or accounting. They are very much drawn to "green issues" and greatly concerned about all humanitarian organizations. This could lead them into politics. Their hobbies tend to be more physical than their jobs. They may be supporters of the local football team, attend classes in martial arts, belong to a tennis club, or be accomplished ballroom dancers.

It is important for a Piscean to do a job that he or she loves. Pisceans are not materialistic or ambitious, so if they work in a secondary position or behind the scenes, they'll be perfectly happy. You'll find Pisces in any organization connected to art or entertainment, particularly film and photography. Many Pisces characters have psychic gifts, and they make excellent counselors. Because this is a water sign, you may find your Pisces partner at a swimming club, at a marina, or fishing beside a river.

How to Please Your Lover

Because Virgo is a perfectionist, you may find it difficult to select an appropriate gift. These people are conservative and detest any hint of vulgarity. Often the wisest choice is to allow them to select their own gift. Do this by offering a gift certificate. They're interested in gardening, so take them to a garden center or give them tickets for a flower show. If you are thinking in terms of jewelry, choose their birthstone—sardonyx.

Capricorn is an earth sign so Capricorns appreciate practical gifts. Good glassware or silver candlesticks will be well received, as will towels or table linen. If they're in business, a handsome leather briefcase or a subscription to the relevant trade magazine will be just right. Don't go overboard with jewelry, but remember that turquoise is their birthstone and that they often prefer silver to gold.

Pisces loves to travel, even if it's only a short trip for a weekend in the country. Choose a lightweight overnight case, folding slippers, or a travel clock to please them. Travel sizes of their favorite (or more expensive) toiletries will also delight them. Even if they're not currently in a position to travel, anything from a faraway place will be gratefully accepted.

Capricorn

December 22 to January 20

Gender: *Feminine/Introvert*
Element: *Earth*
Quality: *Cardinal*
Ruling Planet: *Saturn*

On the day that you were born, the Sun was in the tenth sign of the zodiac, which is Capricorn. This sign is feminine, ruled by Saturn, an earth sign and cardinal in nature. Your symbol is the legendary sea-goat or goatfish. This was a peculiar beast that was half goat and half fish, based on a character called Ea, the ancient god of wisdom. This symbol reflects the complex and thoughtful Capricorn nature.

Capricorn Characteristics

Above all else, Capricorn is ambitious. You don't talk about your aspirations, so others may not be aware that you are something of a high flier. Determined to succeed at anything you undertake, you never miss a trick, seizing every opportunity to advance yourself. If you have role models, they will be self-made successful people whom you admire and wish to emulate. Fortunately, you have a great deal of self-confidence and an unswerving belief in your own abilities.

At the same time, no Capricorn would ever begin a new project without first assessing its true value. You like to take your time before making a commitment. When all these virtues are combined with your capacity for hard work and self-discipline, you can see why success seldom eludes you. The goat is a sure-footed, energetic climber that keeps going until it reaches the top.

You're a good organizer, cautious and realistic, but prepared to take risks if you think it's necessary. Despite your independent streak, you respect authority and appreciate the traditional approach to most aspects of life.

What You Look Like

You will always stand out in a crowd because of your air of assurance. You move swiftly and surely, and obviously know exactly where you are going. Typically, Capricorn has a serious expression, with strong features and a rather formal, old-fashioned manner. Whatever your race, your coloring is possibly rather nondescript and you probably have a prominent nose.

Although you are not overly interested in clothes, you always appear clean and neat, a tendency that increases as you get older. In keeping with your no-nonsense attitude, your color preferences are for the dark and somber shades of gray, brown, navy blue, and black.

Capricorn in Love

Your high standards and your unswerving ambition can present difficulties when you turn your mind to romance. You have trouble expressing your emotions and find it easier to arrange a business seminar than to ask for a date. However, if you can tear yourself away from analyzing your balance sheet for a moment, you may notice that someone is trying to catch your attention. Put your work aside. Try to relax and let your sense of humor come to the surface. Your rare smiles can be extremely attractive.

You will respect your partner and his or her wishes, even if that means keeping your latent passion under firm control. You have distinct and, some would say, old-fashioned views on the sanctity of marriage, clinging to traditional values. Your chosen partner will be one you can look up to, and may be one or two notches higher up the social ladder than you are. You may find, too, that you are drawn to a partner who is a few years your senior.

Because you are always slow to commit yourself, this may take some time. However, don't be tempted to put your love life or your family on hold until you've achieved all your ambitions. You'll always find new heights to scale.

Your Career

Where work is concerned, Capricorns fall into two categories, but both can be found in the world of business rather than in other career areas. The first type is quiet and unassuming, preferring to work behind the scenes on tasks that require precision and attention to detail. Others are great talkers who like to work in sales. Both types have a quick and intuitive mind and can see a trend before it shows itself to others. The world of publishing is full of Capricorns, as it requires someone with business instincts, precision, a love of details, intuition, flare, salesmanship, a liking for people (and gossip), and an interest in art and words. In short, just right for Capricorn!

Your Health

Typical Capricorn trouble spots are the skeleton—particularly the knees—and the skin. Rheumatism or arthritis in the knee joints often causes problems with mobility in later years.

The skin is an excellent barometer of your state of health. It reveals not only your physical condition, but also the state of your mind. If you are worried, stressed, or shocked, you will notice that your skin reacts to this. This reaction varies from person to person. There may be simply a change in the color of the skin, it may become dry and itchy, you may have mild eczema, or you may develop pimples, rashes, or even boils.

Most Capricorns eat a healthy diet and have a definite liking for pasta. This ensures that they remain reasonably slim throughout their lives. Do your best to get some regular exercise to counteract the hours you spend at your desk and to keep your joints moving.

What You Look for in a Partner

As already stated, Capricorn has strong views about marriage. It is not surprising, therefore, that living on love alone doesn't appeal to you. Usually, this means that you will postpone making a firm commitment until you are well established in your career. Some Capricorns do look for money and social status when they are seeking a partner.

You will certainly need someone who is prepared to tolerate your extremely cautious attitude to money—some would call it cheapness. Your partner will need to share your taste for a quiet life, but at the same time will be quite capable of enjoying social events. These are likely to be dinner parties and balls, rather than brunches and disco dances.

Although you will be reluctant to admit it, there are times when you are lacking in self-confidence and easily embarrassed. It's essential, therefore, that your partner be understanding and supportive.

Three Compatible Signs

Scorpio

Scorpio and Capricorn are both highly ambitious and, for this reason, work well together. Sometimes, this partnership starts as a business one; mutual aims and a shared capacity for hard work can often lead to romance. Neither partner will rashly enter into a firm commitment but once the agreement is reached, each will tolerate the others' idiosyncrasies in an attempt to make the relationship work.

Scorpio is passionate and intense about everything. You may find Scorpio's constant digging and delving somewhat trying. They will sincerely rejoice in mutual success, but the Scorpio sting will manifest itself if you succeed where they have failed. The Scorpio jealous streak is something you will need to accept.

Home and family are of primary importance to this sign; Scorpios are completely loyal. Overall, a Capricorn and Scorpio partnership should succeed—but much depends on the business and financial aspects involved.

Cancer

Cancer is your opposite sign. This is an excellent combination, whether the partnership is in business or in love. Indeed, it could cover both aspects of life very happily.

Cancer is moody, but you should understand, because it is a trait that you sometimes share. Like you, Cancerians find it difficult to express emotion, but you will never have reason to doubt their complete loyalty. Be careful not to neglect your Cancer partner because of your devotion to work. Though you won't hear any complaints about it, he or she will notice this and brood about it.

Cancer needs the material things of life in order to feel secure, and you are usually able to provide these. In fact, many Capricorns don't marry until they are well established in business; with Cancer, this works well. A Capricorn-Cancer pairing is usually stable and very happy, particularly if it happens later in life.

Taurus

Taurus is remarkably persistent, and this applies in romance as much as in business. Taureans know exactly what they want and they go after it, no holds barred. Like you, they think hard before making any commitment and, having made it, they will stick by their word, come what may. Once you've committed to a relationship with Taurus, you can forget about escaping from it. What they have, they hold.

Taurus dislikes change, so will enjoy the stability that Capricorn brings to a partnership. Taureans will appreciate your ability to provide a comfortable home, because material possessions are important to them. Their financial aptitude will ensure that money is never a problem.

Taurus is a passionate lover, but don't expect pretty speeches. Taureans show their love by actions, not words. On the rare occasions that they lose their temper, you can witness a truly volcanic Taurean rage. Mercifully, this doesn't happen often. A Capricorn-Taurus partnership is usually blissfully (if silently) happy.

Where to Find Your Partner

If you're looking for a Scorpio partner, you're quite likely to find him or her in medical situations. Scorpios excel as psychiatrists and psychologists because of their love for analysis and investigation. They love attending workshops on self-improvement, witchcraft, psychology, complementary therapies, and mind, body, and spirit subjects, so you will often find them there. On another level, you may be stopped in the street by a Scorpio with clipboard and pen poised, conducting market research. As far as sports are concerned, Scorpio will be found in any game that requires shrewd tactics. You may even find your soul mate on an archaeological dig—such projects are a magnet for Scorpios.

You'll find Cancer in any situation that involves dealing with the public. Cancerians have limitless patience and excel at dealing with irate customers or fractious children. Their affinity with children often leads them into teaching—so keep your eyes open at the next PTA meeting. On the other hand, you may find your partner behind the counter at the corner store. Cancerians like to run their own businesses. Most of them enjoy water sports, such as sailing and swimming, and team games.

Taureans are clever with their hands and have a fine appreciation of design and color. This gives you a clear indication that they are to be found in art groups, craft stores, or do-it-yourself stores. Your own special Taurus may be encountered at concerts or in musical societies. They're often keen gardeners, so seek them out at flower shows or in horticultural societies.

How to Please Your Lover

Scorpio is not easy to please, so beware of buying any gifts at the last minute. They adore presents that evoke the envy of their friends. Be careful to have your gift professionally wrapped. Take your partner to dinner at the best restaurant in town, the one that's booked up for months in advance, and then get the best seats for a new show or a film premiere. Scorpios love special objects, something that is signed by the author or maker or some kind of exclusive find.

Cancerians are generous themselves and genuinely appreciate the same virtue in their partners. The best way to please them is to discover exactly what they really want. Start a casual conversation—they'll realize exactly what you're trying to find out and will (just as casually) give you the information you need. Then, of course, when you hand over your gift, it will be a "big surprise."

Practical Taurus appreciates good quality in useful objects— things like cut-glass dishes or leather desk equipment will please your partner immensely. They're not grasping, but they'd rather have one small, good-quality gift than half a dozen trivial objects. They enjoy their food, so if you've run out of ideas, take them out for a meal, offer a few gourmet treats for their pantry, or hand over a bottle of expensive liquor.

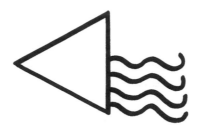

Aquarius

January 21 to February 18

Gender:	*Masculine/Extrovert*
Element:	*Air*
Quality:	*Fixed*
Ruling Planet:	*Uranus*

On the day that you were born, the Sun was in the eleventh sign of the zodiac, Aquarius. This is a masculine air sign. It is ruled by Uranus, the inspirational planet of change. Conversely, Aquarius is a fixed sign, making you strong and dependable. Your astrological symbol is the water carrier, forever giving to others life-sustaining water.

Aquarius Characteristics

Aquarians are certainly unorthodox, and some would say eccentric. With the differing influences in your chart, you can't help but have some contradictory traits. You're an independent thinker and a proponent of speculative ideas who is just as likely to change course in midstream as to see a project through to the end. You claim, though, that you make changes only for a good reason— usually because you've devised a better way of doing things. Anyone who tries to sidetrack you or attempts to tell you what to do will get no sympathy. Your ideas are radical in the extreme, and you do not intend to conform merely because others think you should.

People who don't know you well see you as a dreamer, but you are the sort of person who comes up with dreams that can save the world. You have some truly grandiose ideas, but you hate to be bogged down in the unexciting details. You refuse to recognize any weaknesses—in yourself or your ideas. Such trivialities don't matter when you are involved with matters of great import. When your ideas come to nothing, as they sometimes do, you quickly become disenchanted with everything and everyone. However, this mood is soon forgotten when you come up with an even better brainwave.

You can be unwilling to accept truths that are obvious to others. This trait is good in some ways and bad in others. Colleagues may find it disconcerting but, at the same time, your skepticism can open the way to original ideas, fresh discoveries, and new ways of doing things.

What You Look Like

Your eyes are probably your most outstanding feature. They're likely to be clear, intelligent, and bright. You have a habit of regarding other people with an extremely direct expression, which some may find disturbing. Aquarius is usually slim, with a strong, bony frame and determined jaw. Your hair is unlikely to be your best point, as it is fine and can be unmanageable. Aquarian men tend to lose what little hair they have.

As far as clothes are concerned, you don't much care what you wear. Your taste is definitely individual and you wear what you want, regardless of whether your attire is right for the occasion. Not surprisingly, you like electric blue and other neon colors, but fortunately, the softer shades of turquoise and aquamarine also appeal to you. However, for you, even these more subtle shades can be used to startling effect.

Aquarius in Love

When you fall in love, you'll tend to be even more eccentric. If you make a date, you'll either be late or not show up at all. Your idea of breaking the ice is liable to be a conversation about world affairs, human philosophy, or other abstract topics.

The person who most attracts you will probably be decidedly and obviously unconventional. You soon tire of anyone who appears normal, which to you means dull. Most of the time, you don't even notice that your friends may appear extraordinary to other people; you're happy to take them anywhere.

However, are you willing to commit yourself to a relationship? You enjoy the friendship, but freedom is very important to you. You often avoid one-to-one emotional involvement and, when you do fall in love, you will expect friendship as well as passion. You will be very loyal and faithful—but you'll still demand a great deal of freedom and will expect to be the dominant partner in the relationship.

Your Career

You enjoy working with a group of people, particularly in humanitarian organizations. This type of employment is likely to give you the variety you need. Aquarius dislikes routine and is not at all keen on decision making.

When you're young, you tend to change jobs frequently. You may even dash off to the other side of the world in pursuit of the perfect career. That career needs to involve analysis of some kind, forward thinking, and experimentation. Such requirements could be found in science, charity work, archaeology, or electronics. There are dozens of other jobs, too, in which your many talents can be put to good use. You may even take up astrology—and make a great success of it. If you can find some way of making money while doing what you want, that is the best option for you, because hard work for its own sake bores you to death.

Your Health

Aquarius rules two specific areas of the body: the circulation of the blood and the lower legs. Always buy footwear that gives support to your ankles and be particularly careful in any strenuous activity, such as skiing. The calves are susceptible to two weaknesses, which are night cramps and varicose veins. Both are associated with the circulation of blood in the lower legs. Exercise and massage may alleviate the pain of cramps, though the relief will be only temporary. Varicose veins are a serious matter and, if they develop, you should promptly consult your medical adviser.

The weather always has a profound effect on you. Many natives of this sign suffer from seasonal affective disorder (SAD). Aquarius is usually quite strong, but you do need plenty of exercise, fresh air, and a regular sleeping pattern if you are to remain healthy. You will eat almost anything, so make sure that you follow a sensible diet.

What You Look for in a Partner

You need a partner who is perhaps younger than you. If they appear slightly wild, you'll find them particularly attractive. In fact, anyone who takes on Aquarius must be prepared to expect the unexpected. You're a free spirit, so your partner must be willing to go for a swim at midnight or explore the mountains at dawn, if that takes your fancy.

Your partner will need to be independent and capable of running his or her own life without help from you. Above all, he or she must be prepared to allow you the freedom you need, without protest when you take off alone on some new and exciting project. If your partner can earn enough money (or has inherited enough) to keep both of you so that you don't actually have to work, this is perfect for you.

Aquarius has many friends, and you'll expect your partner to keep an open house for all your slightly weird acquaintances, without comment or criticism. You'll want your partner to take a fair share in the running of the home and, at the same time, to ensure that his or her attitude and personal approach is beyond reproach. All this adds up to a tall order—but then Aquarius can be extremely demanding.

Three Compatible Signs

Aquarius

A partner from your own sign is probably the most compatible choice for you. Aquarius partners are friends as well as lovers. Moreover, you both possess fine minds and enjoy using them. In fact, the intellectual qualities of both partners provide a sound foundation for the success of this relationship. You both enjoy the company of young people, and family is extremely important to you. In this respect, you share similar emotional attitudes that help to make the Aquarius-Aquarius partnership deeply satisfying.

Sagittarius

Sagittarius, like you, has humanitarian and philosophical interests; these establish a strong connection between you. These people are easygoing and helpful—virtues that enable them to cope with Aquarius eccentricities. They're unlikely to make demands and will be happy to allow you as much personal space as you require. They love to talk and will therefore meet all your needs in this direction, particularly insofar as entertaining your friends is concerned. Companionship is an essential part of this relationship, so too many divergent outside interests could cause problems. Overall, though, an Aquarius-Sagittarius pairing can be successful and long-lasting.

Pisces

Pisces and Aquarius combine in a generally harmonious relationship, particularly if Aquarius is the older of the two. You will each be sympathetic to the needs of the other and make a determined effort to ensure that the partnership works. Both are extremely versatile and very concerned for the welfare of others. Pisces is easy to love and responds with deep and demonstrative affection, but problems may arise with the Pisces tendency to moodiness. They're perfectly happy with their own company, but they also need to know that they may come and go as they please— a trait that endears them to freedom-loving Aquarius. An

Aquarius-Pisces partnership can flourish, just as long as Aquarius is sufficiently caring, and shows it.

Where to Find Your Partner

There's no need to tell you where to look for your Aquarius partner. You'll find Aquarians at any of the locations you yourself frequent. If you work as a member of a team or if you belong to any clubs and societies, you could find your partner as a colleague. In short, it's just a question of being on the alert for a fellow Aquarius— though you'll probably be attracted to an Aquarian long before you exchange birth dates.

Sagittarius shares your need for freedom, so it may take you both some time to consider entering into a commitment. These good-humored people love to travel and have an aptitude for foreign languages. Their interests are many and varied, but they have a marked taste for gambling, so you may find them at a casino or a race track.

You could well meet Pisces at a time when you're in trouble, because these sympathetic people love to provide others with a shoulder to cry on. On the other hand, you may find them working for the same humanitarian causes as yourself. They're quiet people, but their steadfast sincerity will be displayed in any emergency or when someone is needed to help with a difficult task.

How to Please Your Lover

Finding the perfect gift for your Aquarius partner will be easy; simply choose something that you would like to receive yourself. It's possible, though, that such accuracy could become boring, so try to produce an item so unusual or beautiful (and, if possible, expensive) that your partner has only dreamed of it. A single orchid in a crystal vase will be sure to please—or consider an old map in an attractive frame. Although you're choosing a gift that you know will please, make an effort to give it a slightly "different" touch.

Because Sagittarius shares so many of your own interests,

you'll assume you'll have no difficulty pleasing your partner. However, remember that your partner's priorities may differ from your own. Try to come up with a gift that will delight your lover— not least because it is something that would not interest you at all. If you're really stumped, produce the very latest book or DVD on one of the hobbies you don't share or suggest a visit to a lecture on some esoteric subject.

Travel is one of the joys you share with Pisces, so you can be sure your partner will be thrilled with a gift from far away. If you're able to afford a short trip abroad, your partner will be ecstatic, but if funds won't stretch that far, think about a visit to somewhere spooky, particularly if it's little known and slightly sinister. Pisces is easily pleased, because it's the thought behind the present rather than the gift itself that most delights.

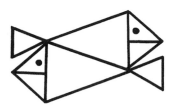

Pisces

February 19 to March 20

Gender: *Feminine/Introvert*
Element: *Water*
Quality: *Mutable*
Ruling Planet: *Neptune*

On the day that you were born, the Sun was in Pisces, the twelfth sign of the zodiac. This is a feminine water sign ruled by the planet Neptune, king of the sea. The old adage that still waters run deep could have been written for you. You certainly have hidden depths and, on occasion, can be remarkably secretive. Your symbol of two fish, joined together but swimming in opposite directions, signals your occasional bouts of perversity. This trait is emphasized by the fact that you are a mutable sign and therefore tend to be changeable.

Pisces Characteristics

The duality of your nature, typified by the two fish tied together, has its benefits and drawbacks. You may set off along a chosen route in life, full of plans and enthusiasm. Then, for no apparent reason, you'll change your mind and take off in the opposite direction. Another of your dual characteristics is that you seem to have the ability to think of two quite unrelated subjects at the same time. Not surprisingly, you bewilder others who cannot follow your train of thought. Hence, you sometimes acquire a reputation for having a grasshopper mind.

Pisces are among the most compassionate people of the zodiac. You possess a natural talent for understanding others. In this respect, you can be almost psychic, often recognizing the problem before you are told what it is. You never hesitate to make personal sacrifices for other people. Your help can take many forms, from a shoulder to cry on and sympathetic advice, to practical help with chores and errands. Beware of allowing yourself to become a martyr to what you think are good causes. You're inclined to be gullible and can be hoodwinked by those who see you as a soft.

You are an optimist and a dreamer, reacting emotionally to everything and everyone. This response can take the form of huge mood swings, a further indication of your dual temperament. Part of you continually wants to go downstream, while the other half struggles to go in the opposite direction.

What You Look Like

Your eyes are probably your most noticeable feature—pale, if you belong to a white race, with heavy lids and a gentle, sympathetic expression. You may curse your thin, flyaway hair. A surprising number of Pisces women wear wigs. You're probably of medium height or a little shorter and may stoop unless you take particular care to stand erect. Slim in youth, you'll probably put on weight as the years pass. Your charming smile lights up your whole face and will soften even the hardest heart.

Pisces loves to be well dressed, and you probably spend a lot of money on your wardrobe. You always buy good-quality clothes and take particular care with your choice of shoes. As far as colors are concerned, you opt for natural shades like cream and taupe or sea greens, blues, and soft gray.

Pisces in Love

You're one of the zodiac's romantics, prone to see the world through rose-tinted glasses. This makes you imagine that every advance made to you will bring your ideal lover. You'll throw caution to the winds if you think that this is the major romance that you've been waiting for. Do try to listen to your intuition. You can be devastated when you are let down.

In any relationship, you're apt to be intensely emotional and submissive. These traits become even more marked when you finally meet the right partner. Nothing is too good for your partner, who can do no wrong.

Because you are such a fantasist, you will willingly enter into a clandestine liaison. To you a secret love affair can be exciting and therefore even more romantic. You'd much rather go out for a candlelit dinner with soft music playing in the background than leap into bed. Cuddling and caressing is often more important to you than the sexual act itself. You can be highly responsive but seldom take the initiative, probably due to your innate shyness.

Pisces loves to be loved. Before you commit yourself to any partnership, be very sure that you are not in love with love itself.

Your Career

Your naturally compassionate temperament, together with a strong sense of service, draws you to those who need help. This opens the door to a wide variety of careers, from caring for children, the sick, the dying, and the elderly, to pastoral work, psychiatry and medicine. Anything that can be considered humanitarian in its widest sense will appeal to you.

You will also be successful in any part of the travel industry and in all aspects of the theater or film work. A number of first-rate actors and writers are Pisceans.

Your Health

Overall, Pisces subjects are healthy people. The feet, including the toes and insteps, are their weakest area, but problems here may not surface until later in life. It makes sense, therefore, always to take particular care of this part of your body. In this way, you may avoid problems with mobility as you get older.

Any reflexologist will remind you that the feet are an excellent barometer of your general health. Pisces may benefit considerably from podiatry and regular reflexology treatments. Your therapist may even be able to pinpoint, from your feet, other areas of your body that need attention.

Pisces usually adopts a practical approach to health and, though you're certainly not a hypochondriac, you will seek advice rather than ignoring any symptoms. At times, you may seem to reel from one minor ailment to another, not feeling ill but definitely less than 100 percent. Watch your diet, get plenty of rest and exercise, and you will find that such incidents are short-lived—unlike Pisces, who tends to reach a ripe old age.

What You Look for in a Partner

An understanding partner is essential if yours is to be a lasting relationship. Pisces is extremely sensitive and easily hurt. You're also susceptible to the pain of others, which makes you doubly vulnerable.

You're idealistic, so your partner will need to sympathize with your views on matters relating to the care of the elderly, child abuse, cruelty to animals, hunting, vivisection, and similar emotional subjects. Your partner will also require a good deal of tact, so he or she they can calm you down when you start agonizing about an item in the newspaper or television news. You need somebody who will be welcoming when you bring home yet another lame dog, and sufficiently practical to cook a meal while you're doing the ministering angel bit.

In addition to all these virtues, your partner needs to be a down-to-earth type, able to deal, kindly but firmly, with your wilder enthusiasms and your occasional deep depressions. Finally, that special person must be sufficiently honest not to take advantage of your submissive tendencies.

Three Compatible Signs
Pisces

Pisces is your ideal partner, so you'll probably recognize each other quickly. The advantage of this union is that you share the same strengths. However, you also have the same weaknesses, and this could mean you'll have problems in coping with the inevitable difficulties of day-to-day living. Certainly, your home is likely to be somewhat chaotic—you're both much too involved with your fantasy world to bother with domesticity. On the plus side, you're unquestionably loyal to each other, and your romantic tendencies could make this a fairy-tale affair. As always, much depends on the other influences in each person's chart, but a Pisces-Pisces pairing is usually happy and successful.

Sagittarius

The attraction between Sagittarius and Pisces is usually instant and powerful. You're both impulsive and likely to be swept away by your feelings. Sagittarius is undemanding in most ways, so will cope happily with the Pisces tendency to live in a dreamworld. Sagittarians be delighted to welcome your friends to the house and, as they share your humanitarian interests, won't object if you tend to turn it into a refuge for waifs and strays of all kinds. A Sagittarius-Pisces relationship can work brilliantly, though sometimes, for no apparent reason, it is not particularly long-lasting.

Aquarius

Aquarius and Pisces have much in common, though this is not immediately obvious. Totally loyal and faithful, both offer the understanding and companionship the other needs. Aquarius can be slightly eccentric and holds some extremely radical convictions, but this won't bother Pisces in the least. Your home will often be filled with a motley crowd of unusual people, and you'll both have a wonderful time dispensing tea and sympathy. An Aquarius-Pisces partnership can be decidedly unconventional but highly successful in its own slightly crazy way.

Where to Find Your Partner

It's highly probable that you'll meet your Pisces partner at a time when one of you needs help. You may both work in some form of social welfare or in a humanitarian field. One of you may be a therapist, adviser, or counselor. You could also meet up at some sort of demonstration, walking side by side in a protest march or at a function for the residents of a retirement center.

Like Pisces, Sagittarius loves anything connected with travel. You could meet your partner when you go to a travel agency or en route to a strange destination with an unpronounceable name. The meeting could take place at a day care center, where one of you is on the staff and the other a parent picking up a child. Sagittarians are obsessive about freedom, so you could find them almost anywhere, but the recognition of a kindred spirit is certain to be mutual.

Strangely, you may know your Aquarius partner already. You have so many interests in common that you probably belong to the same societies or work in the same organization. However, the face Aquarius presents to the world is very different from that of Pisces, so it may take you a while to recognize the rapport between you.

How to Please Your Lover

We have already mentioned the Pisces love for travel and exploration. You should therefore find it easy to choose gifts for your Pisces lover. However, try not to fall into the trap of buying something you can share. You need to make it clear that, no matter how much you have in common, you still regard your partner as an individual. This also applies if you want to buy clothes for your partner. Pisces hates surprises, so take your partner with you to the store to choose what he or she prefers.

Sagittarius will be particularly thrilled with any gift that you yourself have created, be it a hand-knitted sweater or a finely crafted leather wallet. Sagittarians do like a useful gift, such as sports equipment or the latest computer software, but if you're really stumped, they'll be perfectly happy with a gift card.

Aquarius always wants the real thing, so you won't be tempted to offer anything but the best. Aquarians' love for antiques or up-to-date gadgets makes it easy to find an acceptable gift for your partner. Give the selection a good deal of thought, though. These people like to feel that they're important to you and if you offer books or a gift certificate, they may just wonder if it was a last-minute idea.

What You Can Expect from Each Sun Sign

Aries

No secrets or hidden agenda here, as Aries is straightforward. Your Arien lover may be slightly childish at times and may have the occasional temper tantrum.

Taurus

Taureans are financially shrewd, so listen to your partner's advice. They will create a beautiful, comfortable home, but can be obstinate and overpossessive.

Gemini

With a Gemini partner, boredom will be a foreign word. Variety is the spice of a Gemini's life, and they need to be constantly on the move, mentally and physically. Sometimes Gemini is inconsistent and talkative.

Cancer

Your Cancer lover will be intuitive, kind, and helpful. Cancerians are extremely tenacious and highly protective of their loved ones, but can be moody and inclined to self-pity.

Leo

Leos in love are forthright, faithful, and discerning. They will go to almost any length to avenge an injury done to a member of their family. Your Leo partner may be a bit conceited and overbearing.

Virgo

Your Virgo lover may often be critical, but never unkind. These are the perfectionists of the zodiac, particularly insofar as their own behavior is concerned. You may find them finicky and apt to worry about nothing.

Libra

Librans are deeply loving and sensual, cheerful, and usually willing to compromise. They're easygoing and like a quiet life. You may be irritated by their indecision and find their untidiness trying.

Scorpio

Scorpios are totally honest and fair-minded, but they usually get what they want. They have strong feelings about most things, but seldom put them into words. Your lover will be extremely perceptive, but the jealousy and moodiness may be hard to take.

Sagittarius

Sagittarians can be interesting and exciting lovers; your life will not be dull. They are ambitious and versatile, with a strong adventurous streak, but their restlessness and extravagance may trouble you.

Capricorn

Capricorns are great companions, loyal and fun-loving. They're modest, sincere, and good organizers. Their loyalty is unquestionable. However, they're inclined to be wet blankets at times.

Aquarius

Any relationship with Aquarius is likely to be full of surprises. These people are intelligent, eccentric, and erratic. They're highly sexed but make good friends, too. Their lack of tact could cause problems.

Pisces

Intensely emotional, loving, and lovable, your Piscean partner will never let you down. They feel their purpose in life is to fulfill your every need. In time, you may find such adoration too much to handle.

Check Your Compatibility

This chapter lists all the star-sign combinations and gives quick clues to compatibility.

Aries

Aries-Aries

If you're looking for a long-term partnership, this combination could be too hot to handle. It will be exciting while it lasts but could end in fireworks.

Aries-Taurus

This partnership could work if you have interests in common, but Aries may eventually get bored and start playing away from home. Communication is essential to Aries, and that's difficult for Taurus.

Aries-Gemini

Providing Aries can control his or her selfish streak, this pairing could be fantastic.

Aries-Cancer

You're both family oriented, so this relationship could work well, despite the inevitable spats.

Aries-Leo

We find two dominating personalities here, so this is more likely to be a vacation romance than a stable partnership.

Aries-Virgo

There are many differences here but, with mutual respect and a good sex life, this could be a highly satisfactory relationship. If it fails, it will be because Virgo tolerate Aries's domineering attitude.

Aries-Libra

A combination of two cardinal signs doesn't usually last long, because you're both inclined to look elsewhere when the first careless rapture wears off.

Aries-Scorpio

This partnership does work—occasionally. Mostly it falls apart when you eventually get out of bed and try to cope with everyday life. It may be worth trying if true love is there.

Aries-Sagittarius

You're both passionate and sensual, but Sagittarius is often unable to give the emotional support Aries so desperately needs. Even so, if you have shared interests it may work, and the Sagittarian sense of humor will help.

Aries-Capricorn

Capricorn stabilizes Aries, which can be excellent for a business partnership, but two cardinal signs in a personal relationship rarely is a successful combination.

Aries-Aquarius

This pairing often works extremely well because Aquarius ignores Aries's temper tantrums and Aries allows Aquarius the space he or she needs. With a little tolerance from both partners, this relationship could work well.

Aries-Pisces

These people have little in common, but the partnership can be extremely happy. Perhaps it's the attraction of opposites. Pisces looks up to Aries and Aries is enchanted by the gentle Pisces nature.

Taurus

Taurus-Taurus

Much depends here on other factors in the two horoscope charts. It could be a highly successful relationship because you understand each other completely, but the jealous streak in each partner could be your downfall.

Taurus-Gemini

Here, too, you will either complement each other exceptionally well or swiftly learn to detest your partner. Gemini's somewhat fickle attitude will eventually wear down the Taurean's loyalty and dislike of change.

Taurus-Cancer

This may be a slow-growing relationship, but it will be all the better for that. You have a similar outlook on life, so this could well bloom into a strong, long-lasting partnership.

Taurus-Leo

Obstinacy could be the main problem here, because you both tend to be stubborn. Even so, you are both extremely caring, and that very quality could establish the give and take essential to a satisfactory partnership.

Taurus-Virgo

This certainly won't be a peaceful relationship, but it may weather the storms for a while. However, Virgo has a tendency to walk out on Taurus in their middle years.

Taurus-Libra

Libra is laid back and Taurus hates change, so this could be a highly compatible partnership, particularly if you have shared interests.

Taurus-Scorpio

This relationship could be very successful if Scorpio controls his or her selfishness and gives Taurus the support he or she needs. However, you're both very stubborn, which is an obstacle that could lead to disaster.

Taurus-Sagittarius

This partnership is definitely not a good idea unless Sagittarius is allowed to be in charge, and this is unlikely. The Taurus dislike of change and the Sagittarian spirit of adventure could lead to irreconcilable differences.

Taurus-Capricorn
This partnership is better for business than for love, though it can work reasonably well either way. You may both be too stubborn to make a go of it but, if you really care for each other, it will be worth persevering. Much depends on other factors.

Taurus-Aquarius
This is certainly not a love relationship made in heaven, but it could work as a friendship. Taurus will admire many of the Aquarian qualities but will be too down-to-earth for the relationship to survive.

Taurus-Pisces
These two have quite a bit in common and could establish a harmonious relationship based on common interests, particularly in the home, and an unquestioning loyalty.

Gemini

Gemini-Gemini
You are two of a kind, and much depends on other aspects of the charts. You could share a tolerant live-and-let-live attitude, but what happens when you're both demanding attention at the same time? This will be a fragile relationship at best.

Gemini-Cancer
Cancer's nest-making tendencies could provide a loving base for Gemini to return to after you've been off on one of your flighty trips. You could find yourself smothered by Cancer's concern for every aspect of your life or you could love it. Think carefully.

Gemini-Leo
This relationship won't be idyllic—but it could be fun. Gemini will inspire Leo to even greater things. Leo will protect Gemini against all ills. Remember, though, that Leo must be king of the jungle. Look before you leap.

Gemini-Virgo
You have many shared interests, but Virgo's perfectionist streak will almost certainly drive flighty Gemini crazy! Even so, this

partnership could work well. You're both ruled by Mercury so, if problems do arise, you are able to talk about them.

Gemini-Libra

You both expect a great deal from a relationship. Whether or not you get it depends largely on the type of Libran with whom you are involved. There's the potential here for a rewarding partnership, but don't rush into anything.

Gemini-Scorpio

What a sarcastic couple you are! There doesn't seem to be any way this pairing would work. You're both fighting for supremacy with no holds barred. Even so, given some strong aspects in your charts from other signs, it's remotely possible. Don't risk it.

Gemini-Sagittarius

You're on the same level intellectually and share a sense of humor. You're also well matched sexually. Even so, this relationship will probably be more of an intimate, affectionate friendship than a long-lasting love affair.

Gemini-Capricorn

These two make splendid business partners, with Capricorn balancing Gemini's wilder ideas and schemes. It's unlikely that this will develop into a lasting love affair, though, because lighthearted Gemini may well be depressed by Capricorn's dour outlook.

Gemini-Aquarius

Aquarius will be quite content to allow Gemini to float here and there. Gemini will be happy that Aquarius is occupied with saving the world, so won't demand much attention. This could work well—but you're both inclined to the odd extramarital fling.

Gemini-Pisces

This is a workable partnership providing you can both put up with each other's occasional irritating behavior. You both love fantasy, but Gemini may find Pisces too demanding while Pisces may suspect Gemini of infidelity. Even so, you each have qualities the other needs.

Cancer

Cancer-Cancer

Because you're so much alike, this relationship should work, and usually it does. However, your sentimentality could swiftly change to resentment and jealousy at the slightest let-up in demonstrative affection.

Cancer-Leo

There will be frequent battles in this relationship, but it will probably work because both partners love their home and family. Leo is the stronger partner, but Cancer is not entirely averse to being protected and cared for, so things should work well.

Cancer-Virgo

These partners, too, are both family-oriented and therefore reluctant to upset the apple cart. There's a lot of give-and-take in this relationship, with Cancer doing most of the giving, but Cancerians don't mind that.

Cancer-Libra

Both partners have a selfish streak and often bring out the worst in each other. There's a lot of competition here, too, and neither is willing to overlook the other's shortcomings. Overall, these people differ so much that there's little chance of a successful partnership.

Cancer-Scorpio

There's a strong affinity between the crab and the scorpion, and it could develop into a harmonious relationship. Cancer needs to control his or her possessive nature, and Scorpio must refrain from stinging remarks in any confrontation. Keep romance alive and this pairing could work well.

Cancer-Sagittarius

This is sometimes a love-at-first-sight affair, but it's unlikely to last. Sagittarius must have freedom and Cancer won't permit it. Additionally, Sagittarius may be tried beyond endurance by Cancer's tendency to whine.

Cancer-Capricorn

This can be one of the most successful pairings in the zodiac, particularly if it's a second marriage for either partner. Capricorns are a hard worker, and, by the time they marry for the second time, they're likely to be on a firm footing financially. This suits Cancer admirably, and the result is likely to be a superb partnership.

Cancer-Aquarius

These two find it difficult to understand each other, which means that the initial strong sexual attraction soon fades. Cancer won't appreciate the Aquarian tendency to act on impulse, and Aquarius will lose patience with Cancer's worrying nature.

Cancer-Pisces

Both of these people are exceptionally sensitive, so they go to great lengths to avoid hurting each other. In other ways, they may seem an oddly matched couple for a variety of reasons, but their partnership is likely to be harmonious and lasting.

Leo

Leo-Leo

Two Leos can blend happily, but it's not easy. They're both fiery, so there's plenty of passion in the relationship. Both like the limelight, so there is constant rivalry. Even so, this partnership can work—in a crazy, tumultuous sort of way.

Leo-Virgo

Both parties have clear ideas of what they expect from a relationship, and they do their best to achieve it. Virgo may be a little too cool for Leo, but they compromise and the pairing often works well.

Leo-Scorpio

The initial attraction here is strong and immediate, but Leo's roar and Scorpio's sting can cause problems. It seems an unlikely combination, but for some reason this match is often successful.

Leo-Sagittarius
Two fire signs here provide a highly combustible situation. Both have tremendous drive and both are strongly sexed. They're a tough couple and can often make a successful partnership, apparently against all odds.

Leo-Capricorn
This partnership works well when there is mutual respect and a shared business interest. Leo can be upset by Capricorn's detached approach, but they have complementary traits that provide a strong basis for a good partnership.

Leo-Aquarius
These two powerful and obstinate people don't often make a successful pairing. Both of these are fixed signs who don't part easily once they have made a commitment, so this could lead to a long and difficult relationship. However, if other factors on their charts add adaptability and good humor, it can work.

Leo-Pisces
This combination has the greatest chance of success if the Leo is male and older than Pisces. Both signs are creative and enjoy a glamorous lifestyle, so this could work well if Pisces is content to allow Leo to be the dominant partner.

Virgo

Virgo-Virgo
As always with same-sign pairings, this can be delightful or disastrous. The main danger lies in the constant nitpicking criticism natural to this sign. If both partners have absorbing but separate interests outside the home, this relationship could work well.

Virgo-Libra
These two have a number of likes and dislikes in common. They're both cool customers, able to stand back from any problems. Virgo will find it difficult to get Libra to make a decision, but even so, this partnership could succeed.

Virgo-Scorpio

This isn't usually a successful partnership. Scorpio bullies Virgo. Virgo irritates Scorpio. They try hard to present a united front, but the result is unlikely to be a lasting partnership.

Virgo-Sagittarius

Virgo is inclined to be standoffish and introverted. Sagittarius loves to be at the center of everything. Their divergent interests could cause problems. However, they share a sense of humor, so the attraction of opposites may make a happy relationship.

Virgo-Capricorn

These people have a great deal in common, and this should be a remarkably sound relationship, particularly if they are in business together. They're a levelheaded couple, and mutual respect ensures that this partnership is practically indestructible.

Virgo-Aquarius

This is a case of marry in haste, repent at leisure. Initially, everything in the Virgo-Aquarius garden is lovely, but the partners demand too much of each other and the relationship is unlikely to last.

Virgo-Pisces

This is another case of the attraction of opposites. Virgo is grounded and stable, well able to support dreamy, watery Pisces. Providing Pisces is not too untidy and disorganized, this partnership should succeed.

Libra

Libra-Libra

These are two well-balanced people here, so this should be a partnership based on common sense and harmony. The Libran reputation for placidity is not always accurate, and there can be some problems if aggression rears its ugly head. Both find it difficult to reach a decision about anything, which doesn't help.

Libra-Scorpio

Libra sometimes finds Scorpio too possessive, and Scorpio becomes impatient with Libra's slowness. There's a hint of jealousy here, too, and sparks can fly—often without justification.

Libra-Sagittarius

There's always a strong attraction here, but it sometimes wears off quite quickly. Both have a sense of humor and are good companions. This match should work well, providing there are no money worries.

Libra-Capricorn

This makes a wonderful business partnership but is a little detached for a permanent liaison. Capricorn often looks for a younger partner, and there is a strongly protective feeling to the relationship.

Libra-Aquarius

A Libra-Aquarius partnership can be one of the best in the zodiac. Neither party is possessive, but Libra is inclined to sulk at times.

Libra-Pisces

There is usually a strong physical attraction between these two, and the early days of the relationship can be ecstatic, sexually and emotionally. However, both signs are easily hurt and disillusion can set in after a while.

Scorpio

Scorpio-Scorpio

These two strong characters can have a stormy yet compatible relationship. They know each other's weaknesses and have no hesitation in taking advantage of them—yet they enjoy the battles and often achieve a mutual respect that keeps them together for years.

Scorpio-Sagittarius

This pairing is certainly not ideal, yet it can last for a long time because both signs are always hoping that things will improve. They tend to expect too much from the relationship and from each other.

Scorpio-Capricorn
As far as these two are concerned, the initial attraction can be based
on a mutual aim to achieve something. Capricorn can stand up to
Scorpio and has the patience to wait for love and companionship.
Eventually, this is a happy mating.

Scorpio-Aquarius
Both these signs are obstinate and tense. Aquarius is blunt, and
Scorpio resents this. As a result, this relationship is usually an
ongoing pitched battle. There seems little point in even trying to
build a partnership.

Scorpio-Pisces
In marked contrast to the two previous signs, Scorpio and Pisces
have every chance of making a harmonious relationship. Both are
emotional and intuitive and go to great lengths to keep each other
happy.

Sagittarius

Sagittarius-Sagittarius
Sagittarius is ruled by benevolent Jupiter, and this alone ensures
that this match will be happy. These partners are determined to
enjoy a successful relationship. The only possible snag could be
that they are too similar for comfort.

Sagittarius-Capricorn
These two signs have little in common, yet this can sometimes be a
successful relationship. Sagittarius inspires Capricorn to take a
lighter approach than usual, and Capricorn is able to steady
Sagittarius's wilder flights of fancy.

Sagittarius-Aquarius
This should be a good match. Both partners are independent and
intelligent and share a conviction that a permanent relationship
must be worked at.

Sagittarius-Pisces
These two signs have much in common, though there are also a
number of differences. More than anything else, shared spiritual

interests will cement the bond between them and result in a loving relationship.

Capricorn

Capricorn-Capricorn
Two Capricorns in one household will likely result in a tranquil atmosphere. They understand each other perfectly. Both are hard workers and, once their goals have been defined, they will work toward them steadily.

Capricorn-Aquarius
This is a relationship in which the partners regard each other as equals. They share a desire to do some good in the world. Both signs are determined to get the best from their lives together, and they can prove indomitable.

Capricorn-Pisces
Pisces has a dreamy, idealistic nature that arouses all the Capricorn protective instincts. When Capricorn gets moody, Pisces remains calm and unruffled. This couple can be very compatible and enjoy a wonderfully happy relationship.

Aquarius

Aquarius-Aquarius
Anything can happen in this weird and wonderful match, and both partners will revel in the uncertainty. Both are highly intelligent and great talkers. Only if this communication ceases will there be any risk of parting. Usually, this relationship is stimulating, affectionate, and long-lasting.

Aquarius-Pisces
This partnership is based on sympathetic understanding of each other and a genuine desire to please. It works best if Aquarius realizes that Pisces needs constant reassurance of being loved.

Pisces

Pisces-Pisces

Friends are likely to consider this couple to be joined at the hip. They dislike being apart and never tire of showing their love for each other. Facing up to the realities of earning a living, washing the dishes, and bringing up children can be worrying, but their devotion will usually see them through any difficulties.

Moon Signs

Introduction

The zodiac sign occupied by the Moon at the time of your birth is known as your Moon sign. This shows your inner, emotional side and it can give far more information about a person's basic or real needs than the Sun sign.

Choosing a partner will always be a primarily emotional matter. It's therefore important for you to be aware of your potential lover's characteristics. In this respect, your Moon sign and that of your prospective partner could be of the greatest significance, even more so than the Sun sign or the rising sign.

Finding a Moon Sign

The following charts will enable you to determine the Moon sign for yourself or anyone else.

First, look at the Year section of the large table and find your year of birth. Track to the right along the same line, into the Month section until you reach your birth-month column. Note down the zodiac sign where the line and the column cross.

Next, look at the smaller table headed Exact Day of Birth, and find the day of the month on which you were born. The number immediately below it is the number of zodiac signs you must add to the zodiac sign you have noted down to reach your Moon sign. For example, if you were born on November 5, 1975, your Moon sign works out to be Libra plus the next two signs, Scorpio and Sagittarius; in other words, Sagittarius.

YEAR					MONTH											
					JAN	FEB	MAR	APR	MAY	JUN	JUL	AUG	SEP	OCT	NOV	DEC
1920	1939	1958	1977	1996	Tau	Can	Can	Vir	Lib	Sag	Cap	Aqu	Ari	Tau	Can	Leo
1921	1940	1959	1978	1997	Lib	Sco	Sag	Cap	Aqu	Ari	Tau	Can	Leo	Vir	Sco	Sag
1922	1941	1960	1979	1998	Aqu	Ari	Ari	Gem	Can	Leo	Vir	Sco	Cap	Aqu	Ari	Tau
1923	1942	1961	1980	1999	Gem	Leo	Leo	Lib	Sco	Cap	Aqu	Ari	Tau	Gem	Leo	Vir
1924	1943	1962	1981	2000	Sco	Sag	Cap	Aqu	Ari	Tau	Gem	Leo	Lib	Sco	Sag	Cap
1925	1944	1963	1982	2001	Pis	Tau	Tau	Can	Leo	Lib	Sco	Sag	Aqu	Pis	Tau	Gem
1926	1945	1964	1983	2002	Leo	Vir	Lib	Sco	Sag	Aqu	Pis	Tau	Can	Leo	Vir	Lib
1927	1946	1965	1984	2003	Sag	Cap	Aqu	Pis	Tau	Gem	Leo	Vir	Sco	Sag	Aqu	Pis
1928	1947	1966	1985	2004	Ari	Gem	Gem	Leo	Vir	Sco	Sag	Aqu	Pis	Ari	Gem	Can
1929	1948	1967	1986	2005	Vir	Sco	Sco	Cap	Aqu	Pis	Tau	Gem	Leo	Vir	Lib	Sag
1930	1949	1968	1987	2006	Cap	Pis	Pis	Tau	Gem	Leo	Vir	Sco	Sag	Cap	Pis	Ari
1931	1950	1969	1988	2007	Tau	Can	Can	Vir	Lib	Sag	Cap	Pis	Ari	Gem	Can	Leo
1932	1951	1970	1989	2008	Lib	Sag	Sag	Aqu	Pis	Tau	Gem	Can	Vir	Lib	Sag	Cap
1933	1952	1971	1990	2009	Pis	Ari	Tau	Gem	Can	Vir	Lib	Sag	Cap	Aqu	Ari	Tau
1934	1953	1972	1991	2010	Can	Vir	Vir	Lib	Sag	Cap	Pis	Ari	Gem	Can	Vir	Lib
1935	1954	1973	1992	2011	Sco	Cap	Cap	Pis	Ari	Gem	Can	Vir	Sco	Sag	Cap	Aqu
1936	1955	1974	1993		Ari	Tau	Gem	Leo	Vir	Lib	Sco	Cap	Pis	Ari	Tau	Can
1937	1956	1975	1994		Leo	Lib	Lib	Sag	Cap	Pis	Ari	Tau	Can	Leo	Lib	Sco
1938	1957	1976	1995		Cap	Aqu	Pis	Ari	Tau	Can	Leo	Lib	Sco	Cap	Aqu	Ari

Naturally, this is not an exact system, but it is accurate enough for most people and it will certainly do until you have a full natal chart to look at.

EXACT DAY OF BIRTH							
1	**2**	**3**	**4**	**5**	**6**	**7**	**8**
0	1	1	1	2	2	3	3
9	**10**	**11**	**12**	**13**	**14**	**15**	**16**
4	4	5	5	5	6	6	7
17	**18**	**19**	**20**	**21**	**22**	**23**	**24**
7	8	8	9	9	10	10	10
25	**26**	**27**	**28**	**29**	**30**	**31**	
11	11	12	12	1	1	2	

The Moon Through the Signs

Moon in Aries

Strong emotional responses, which can sometimes lead to impetuous behavior, are typical of Moon in Aries subjects. Power is important to you, and you expect to be the leader in any situation. This urge to be in charge and to solve problems as soon as they arise means that you often upset other people with your high-handed attitude. Your enthusiasm can make you unrealistic, and you quickly become bad-tempered if others don't agree with you. The combination of the feminine Moon tendencies with the fiery Aries temperament can cause tension within yourself and in your dealings with other people.

As far as romance is concerned, you're something of a flirt, enjoying many a quick fling before you settle down. You may have a taste for partners younger than yourself, because you find them more malleable than people in your own age group. A permanent relationship will not be a priority for you. You'll be in no hurry to enter into the demands and responsibilities involved in such a partnership. Then, one day, you'll suddenly feel lonely. That's when you'll begin to think that settling down is not such a bad idea after all.

Problems with choosing a permanent partner could arise if your own family background was unhappy. The problems encountered then could be paralleled in later life, making it difficult for you to establish lasting relationships.

You're a deep thinker, and first impressions mean a lot to you. In fact, Moon in Aries subjects are often attracted to uniforms, so the person who catches your eye could be anyone from a nurse to a regular soldier. When you do meet somebody special, you may fall head over heels in love, but you still prefer your potential partner to make the first move. You're extremely demanding and not always easy to live with. Your partner will need to be independent yet always willing to fall in with your plans and ideas. New projects, constant change, and excitement are necessary for you. There's no way you could endure a partner who is constantly complaining and emotional. Should your intuition warn you that you've made a mistake, you'll display your usual lack of finesse and quit, probably leaving your partner to nurse a broken heart.

Even after you have made a commitment, you may still have a roving eye. You have no hidden agendas, but you can be on an emotional seesaw so that your partner doesn't always know what to expect of you. You are not good at concealing your inconsistent behavior, and confrontation can sometimes lead to temper tantrums that you later regret.

The unpredictable Moon in Aries nature cuts both ways when it comes to finding a lover. On the negative side, you're always on the run, seeking new pastures, traveling for the sake of it. Who can catch you when you're here one moment and gone the next? More positively, your restlessness ensures that you meet many people. With any luck, you'll one day bump into the one person who is absolutely right for you. When that happens, your Aries determination will come into play and you'll have no hesitation at all about choosing your lover.

Moon in Taurus

The Moon in Taurus makes you keep your emotions under tight control. Emotional satisfaction, for you, is found in the security of a stable home and material possessions. You enjoy a steady pace in everything and hate change, to the extent that it can really frighten you. Taurus is an earth sign, so you center your life on home, family, and the pets that you are sure to have. Although you're quiet and reserved, you have a strong character and cope well when disaster strikes. You're extremely tenacious and sometimes obstinate, and you will battle through any hardships without complaint. You seldom show hurt feelings or resentment openly but very occasionally and under great provocation, your Taurus temper will let fly.

One of the things you most fear is poverty. The idea of having a partner who is financially dependent on you makes you cringe. How could you possibly risk losing your wonderful home, or having to lower your standard of living? You like the good things in life, and a wealthy lover comes high on the list, but not even your worst enemy could describe you as avaricious. Money and possessions are important to you because they represent security.

These characteristics make it difficult for you to become emotionally involved on a purely romantic basis. You really fear that this person may become a parasite, draining you financially and leaving you destitute. There's no way of insuring against such problems and, oddly enough, if the worst does happen, you'll simply set about rectifying the situation. Even so, discovering that your loved one has the Midas touch will certainly help to fire your passion.

The good news is that once you've found your soul mate, rich or poor, you'll be transformed. Having committed yourself to a partnership, you will be unstintingly caring and completely faithful. You are extremely sensuous and demonstrative but often too inhibited to make the first move. You are touchy-feely and need a lover who responds in similar fashion. Lacking this, you'll withdraw into your shell, becoming silent and unhappy.

It is important that you find a partner who, like you, can appreciate all five senses. Does he love gourmet meals? Will she enjoy listening to soft, tender music while cuddling up in front of a log fire? Can he weep at an emotional film? You need a partner who can share your feelings about these seemingly trivial matters.

When the right person for you does come along, you will take time to make up your mind. However attractive that person seems, you will be afraid of making a mistake and of losing everything you have worked for. Only when you feel safe with the person in question will you take the plunge and be willing to gamble everything on the partnership. Then you will demonstrate complete loyalty to the love of your life and defend your relationship against all comers.

Moon in Gemini

Your attitude to relationships takes a lot of understanding. For instance, it takes you a long time to choose a partner and to make a commitment, but when you do so, you don't hold back. This said, there are aspects of your personality, opinions, and ideas that you prefer not to share, so your commitment may look deep, all-powerful, and permanent, but this is not the case. If you become really fed up, you can walk out without looking back.

You find it difficult to handle deep emotions and are therefore inclined to trivialize them. If you find yourself out of your depth in an emotional situation, you could well become irritable. You have a restless nature, and most people see you as something of a social butterfly. If you find yourself living with someone who is awash with emotion or unable to express what is going on in his or her mind, you will try to make the relationship work, but if you can't, then you will give up on it.

Your chosen partner will have to be mentally stimulating as well as being witty and interesting. You do tend to accept a person at face value, so beware of being tricked by someone who has more wiles than you do. Once you recognize such a situation, you'll be off like a shot, but it could still be a trying experience.

Communication is the essence of life to you, and you will be happiest with someone who is not too shy to tell you that they love you. Don't make any commitment until you are sure that your chosen partner is willing to work out any problems that may arise by talking them through. You're not the type who likes to keep your worries to yourself, though you can be most helpful if your partner—or anyone else—is upset. You have an inborn ability to pick up the vibes when anyone is distressed. You're not the most reliable of partners and can swiftly become bored with a permanent relationship. However, the time may come when it is your partner who calls it off. Only then will you realize exactly how important that person is to your life.

Moon in Cancer

The moon is Cancer's ruling planet and, because it controls the inner you, you will be more emotionally sensitive than most. You are capable of great depth and intensity of feeling, but tend to hold back when meeting strangers until you are sure of the people concerned. Home and family are of primary importance to you, particularly as far as children are concerned. You hate the idea of leaving your family home and striking out on your own. In this respect, you're rather like the hermit crab: so you won't move from the safety of one home until you're convinced of the security of the next.

You are highly sensitive to the feelings of others and find it easy to make friends with life's rejects and with the underdogs of society. You're always ready to listen to a sob story and lend a helping hand. Some people may consider you a gullible but, fortunately, you're quick to detect insincerity and will scuttle away before you get hurt.

You have no difficulty in attracting the opposite sex, but when it comes to choosing a lover, you are almost excessively cautious. You're extremely shy and find it difficult to show your feelings. Additionally, you're inclined to be moody, and it's not always easy to understand your occasionally erratic behavior. You'll be scared off by anyone who's looking for a short-term fling. However, your intuition will swiftly warn you if not all is well. Above all else, you need security, so this will be your primary demand of any partner. You also need someone who understands and shares your sensitivity.

If you are let down, you'll swiftly return to the family home for help, and it may be some time before you risk venturing out again. When the right partner does come along, you'll be reliable and completely faithful, doing your best to forget painful past experiences. You're a natural homemaker and will enjoy building your own love nest.

Men who have the Moon in Cancer subconsciously look for a partner who will be a mother substitute or someone who will comfort and care for. She'll be the girl-next-door type, of whom your mother would approve. If you're a woman you'll seek out a partner who can fulfill your romantic fantasies and provide the dream home in which you can settle down to rear your own family.

Don't be afraid to use your innate intuitive powers to help you find the partner you want. Your natural instincts seldom let you down, and though it may take some time, the right person for you will come along. When that happens, the relationship is likely to be permanent. You're a faithful type and, additionally, you have a strongly possessive streak and hate to end a relationship. It is worth remembering, though, that you always demand your own space. Your partner will need to appreciate this and show understanding when you sometimes withdraw into your shell.

Moon in Leo

If you were born with the Moon in the sign of Leo, you're likely to be the star of any undertaking with which you are associated. This suits you very well, because you take it for granted that you're someone rather special. No matter what you undertake, you do it with flair, energy, and pride. You also expect that your unusual talents will be recognized and applauded. If they're not, you sulk or throw a tantrum.

You're confident that you know best, whatever the situation, and this can lead to you handing out too much unsolicited advice. It's also well nigh impossible for you to accept orders. Indeed, you take it for granted that other people will follow where you lead and, if you lead them over the edge of the precipice—well, obviously that's their fault, not yours.

You have a highly emotional nature and attract the opposite sex like bees to honey. Whoever heard of a Moon in Leo lacking admirers? You're a romantic at heart and, in truth, are at your happiest when you're in love. It's essential, though, that your partner admire and respect you. Potential partners also need to be aware of what makes you tick; otherwise your self-centered attitude will quickly scare them away.

You'll certainly choose a partner of whom you can be proud, just as long as he or she doesn't try to usurp your center-stage position. If your partner flatters you—which he or she will do if he or she really understands you—you'll purr with satisfaction. Deep down you fear criticism, mainly because you don't know how to handle it, and you usually feel it's unjustified anyway.

Once you enter into a commitment, your generosity will come to the fore and you'll shower your partner with gifts, making it clear that what's yours is also your partner's. This is fine until you go over the top and spend more money than you have. Your love of the good things in life can all too easily empty your pockets.

At the deepest level, you always did think of yourself as a deity, and now you are willing to elevate someone else to share your pedestal. However, this brings an unforeseen downside. It gives you power over your partner—and for you power and love are equally important. A word of warning is appropriate here, as you must avoid being arrogant and overbearing. If you don't, you'll end up a lonely Leo, wondering where you went wrong.

The Moon in Leo also influences another aspect of your love life. Children draw you like a magnet. You enjoy making them happy and you're the ideal person to run a children's party. The youngsters, too, identify with your childlike sense of fun. If a child is in tears, you'll be the first to offer comfort. Make sure that your partner shares your love for children and is willing to start a (large) family. The Moon in Leo may not be satisfied with a childless relationship.

Moon in Virgo

As the Moon was in the sign of Virgo when you were born, you have a tendency to allow your head to rule your heart. You also appear to be shy and retiring, lurking in the background, weighing people up and evaluating them.

You tend to be a perfectionist, though, to be fair, you are just as demanding of yourself as you are of others. This urge for perfection makes you extremely critical, and you're often convinced that you're the only person who can do a job properly. Then you become desperately worried in case you fail. Fortunately, this doesn't often happen, because you combine high intelligence with a marked practical streak.

Are you going to be too choosy and demand that your mate be perfect in your eyes? This is unlikely, to say the least. However, an even worse scenario would be to settle for second best. Why would you do this? You'll be confident that you can correct your partner's deficiencies. Beware of trying to dictate the terms of your relationship—it seldom works.

What do you look for in a partner? Potential partners must share your high standards of personal hygiene. They must be neat and tidy and never disturb your orderly approach to every aspect of life. If you can find someone whose own environment is as organized and meticulous as your own, your dreams may come true. When it comes to weighing up the pros and cons of the relationship, as you surely will, this fastidiousness will give them a very big plus.

It's important that your partner should love animals as much as you do. For you, a meeting in the park while you are both walking your pets is definitely a good starting point. This could even initiate a romance.

You have a tendency to attract every lame dog around— parasites who are interested only in their own agendas and what they can get out of you. Fortunately, you're usually quick to recognize these people. Even so, it's possible that you could initially be deluded at the start of a love affair and then, in true

Moon-in-Virgo style, you'll feel guilty when you end the relationship.

In general, your greatest need is to stop seeing everything as black or white. Learn to accept some gray areas. When you meet a possible partner, try to accept what you see as their imperfections. Hopefully, your potential mate will also overlook your weaknesses, so that you can have a good chance of establishing a positive relationship.

Moon in Libra

With the Moon in Libra, you need harmony in every aspect of your life. You just can't cope with any form of dissension and, in fact, conflict is actually bad for your health. On the other hand, you do enjoy a little excitement and derive a great deal of satisfaction from creating calm out of chaos.

You're an ambitious person, full of ideas and determined to put them into practice. The problem is that though you're great on theory, you are not so good at making things happen. You need other people—colleagues, friends, and partners—to help you achieve the balance that is so essential to you.

It may seem out of character, but lunar Librans adore speed in any form, particularly as far as cars are concerned. You're also clever with intricate machinery. You have tremendous empathy with weak people, children, and the elderly and are quick to notice any signs of stress in a friend or partner.

Your easy, affable manner attracts many friends of the opposite sex, and you're content to maintain those friendships at an intellectual level. You are more at ease keeping your friends at arm's length rather than holding them in your arms. Some people may misunderstand your rather detached manner and consider you unfeeling.

For you, genuine platonic relationships are the order of the day, until the right person comes along. Even then, you may fail to recognize them. When you have the Moon in Libra, you often need a gentle push from a third party who can see, more clearly than you do, that your destiny has arrived. You are aware of this tendency and usually rely on one close friend and confidant to help you in these matters.

You can't circumvent your indecisiveness; it's part of your nature. However, before committing yourself to a relationship you must ensure that your partner understands you completely and is prepared to accept you just as you are. At the same time, don't expect any relationship to be all sweetness and light. Your perfect partner needs a harmonious home. At the same time, like you, your partner will appreciate a little excitement. You should be prepared to allow the scales to tip down on one side or the other occasionally. If you sit on the fence too often, you may drive your partner to despair, and they'll send you packing.

Your ideal partner will have class. You need someone tactful, intelligent, and kind, who will be a social asset. This paragon also needs to be extremely companionable, as you hate to be alone. You need someone who will share your taste in music and your leisure interests. If, like you, your partner is well mannered, elegant, and quietly self-confident, you're likely to be known as the happiest couple in town.

Moon in Scorpio

The Moon in Scorpio produces a positive, determined, and confident character. You have a quick temper but are unfailingly caring to the important people in your life. Sometimes, the contradictory aspects of your character make you difficult to understand. You dislike change yet also enjoy taking up an exciting challenge. You are content to remain in the same job and house for years but will then suddenly decide that change is the order of the day.

You can be jealous and possessive at times, but only if you have some reason for feeling insecure. Sometimes, too, you tend to hold a grudge for years and, eventually, to seek revenge. On the other hand, you will always remember a kindness and ensure that generosity is rewarded.

Moon-in-Scorpio subjects hate to appear foolish. The face you present to the world is dignified, sober, and self-possessed. This may give the impression that you're cold and uncaring; however, at home with your beloved family, you are a different person—fun-loving, gentle, and affectionate.

Deep down, you believe that somewhere in the world there is one person who was meant for you, perhaps a soul mate from a previous life. A harmonious and lasting relationship is something that you may strongly desire but achieve only with difficulty. In fact, you may experience massive heartbreak before you find your one true love. You above all others feel everything so intensely that when a love affair goes wrong you are totally devastated and inconsolable for a while. However, you're also a survivor. In time, you will pick up the threads of your life again; then, when you're least expecting it, the right person will suddenly appear to compensate for all the previous heartache.

This doesn't mean that everything is coming up roses. Before either one of you enter into that much-desired commitment, some honest discussion is called for. Moon-in-Scorpio people have a dark side, and you must be sure that your partner is aware of this. Don't worry too much. Every Moon sign has its faults. Just admit to your partner that at times you can be unyielding, suspicious, and morose.

Moon in Sagittarius

When you were born, the Moon was in Sagittarius, imparting a cheerful, optimistic nature to someone who cannot bear to be pinned down, either physically or mentally. Greener pastures always attract you, whether it is to explore a neighboring state or the latest religious belief.

Although you have a restless temperament, you still need a home base; this is important to you. It is a place where you can relax on the rare occasions when you need to recoup your strength (or your finances). Even so, you could well become bored and be up and away again within a few days.

New ventures hold tremendous appeal, so perhaps this time you'll realize those idealistic dreams. The problem with this aspect of your personality is that it encourages you to speak before you think, and you can land in some dicey situations as a result.

With the Moon in Sagittarius, you're a charismatic type; you will certainly not lack admirers. This can mean that you imagine yourself in love several times before the right person comes along. Your friends would say that you have itchy feet, and it's true that you scarcely have time to get to know anyone before you're taking off for a new destination. This restlessness can cause problems when you're looking for a long-term relationship.

Your partner will obviously need to be an adventurous type and will almost certainly love the outdoors. He or she will have to respect your need for freedom and allow you to exercise it whenever you wish. Oddly enough, once you have found this paragon, you will no longer be so obsessed with independence. Why? Because you now have choice, and that in itself is freedom.

In line with your own positive, cheerful nature, you will want a partner who is capable of enjoying life to the fullest and who has a great sense of humor. Your Sagittarian Moon ensures that your partner's nationality, creed, or color will not concern you in the least.

It may take you some time to make up your mind about forming a permanent relationship, because you are hesitant about being tied down. For this reason, you're likely to form your partnership later in life than the average. You'll probably have several halfhearted affairs, because you're an inveterate suitor. In fact, it can sometimes seem that you prefer the chase.

However, eventually you'll find your lover, one who will follow you to the ends of the earth, if necessary, and enjoy sharing your new experiences. Then you'll wake up to the fact that you've found not only a lover but also a friend who will be your constant companion.

Moon in Capricorn

If you were born with the Moon in Capricorn, you'll be loyal, caring, and devoted to your family. You're ambitious, and you like to hold a position of authority, but strangely, this placement means you lack self-confidence. You're shy, too, and keep your emotions under strict control, so much so that you sometimes appear cold and uncaring.

If you run your own business, you're likely to be successful. Moon-in-Capricorn people enjoy being self-employed and have the discipline to cope with it. Security is important to you, and you're the sort of person who becomes a regular saver early in life. You have a particularly practical approach to everything and like to plan ahead, never acting on impulse.

You are cautious about entering into new relationships. Your shyness makes it difficult for you to ask for a date, and you don't form liaisons lightly. For you, life is a serious matter in all its aspects, and romance is no exception. Those with the Moon in Capricorn do not flirt, and they will only give way to an outburst of emotion when under great stress. In some respects, you can be very cynical about love and will need to overcome this if you are to find your perfect partner.

You are fearful of rejection, and this makes you all the more cautious in your approach to the person you are interested in. You hide behind a brusque manner that is unlikely to attract people. Having gotten up the nerve to make an approach, you may then get cold feet and draw back. The strange thing is that you don't seem to realize that this excessive caution is part of your nature. Instead, you become convinced that no one will ever love you because you are in some way inferior. This in turn makes you even more cautious, so that choosing your lover carefully takes on a different meaning for you. You could decide, quite rationally, to choose a partner who will provide a home and domestic security. In short, you'll settle for a business relationship and eschew romance.

However, there is no need to do this. You can find your genuine soul mate, should you continue to look for one. This ideal mate is someone who feels the same way as you do, who is equally shy, and who seeks a partner who is absolutely loyal and faithful. When you meet this person, you will both feel free to express your feelings, without shyness or reserve. In fact, you'll go to great lengths to reassure each other that this is important, and that your motives are pure and true. You will also give each other that all-important assurance of security that has hitherto been lacking in your life.

If you are still young, it's probable that your soul mate will be several years older than you are. If you're already a senior citizen and have not found your ideal partner, don't despair. It's never too late to find your true love and, when you do, the waiting will have been well worthwhile.

Moon in Aquarius

An Aquarian Moon makes you cool and detached, but unable to understand your own emotions. Because of this inner conflict, you find it difficult to show your feelings, leaving others to wonder whether you are shallow. The truth is that your emotions are buried deep, and it takes something special to make them surface.

You have a vast range of friends and are able to relate happily to all social groups. Some people think it odd that you'll befriend the bum on the sidewalk when you're on your way to have dinner at the Ritz with an heiress. They simply fail to understand that in your eyes the bum and the heiress are both part of humankind, as you are, and therefore deserving of the same respect. You prefer to be with a group of people rather than in a one-on-one situation. In a group, you are completely at ease and can allow your natural sense of humor to surface.

One characteristic of the Moon in Aquarius is that you are often drawn to people who have already made a commitment. Eventually, though, it could be one of your group of friends who introduces you to the person you are looking for—the perfect partner. This will probably be someone younger than you are—someone who is lively, optimistic, and impulsive.

Above all else, you need a lover who is also a friend. For both of you, friendship is the foundation for love and, indeed, deepens your mutual esteem. This person will be intelligent, strong-willed, and independent and will share your unconventional attitudes. They will also recognize your need for personal space and won't be perturbed if you suddenly depart on solitary trips to unnamed destinations.

This inborn quality of detachment makes you shy away from anyone who is overly emotional or touchy-feely, particularly at the start of a relationship. Intellectual rapport may come, given time. Physical intimacy takes much longer to develop. Even so, once you have made a commitment to each other, your sex life with your partner can be amazing!

Your ability to stand back and make a dispassionate assessment can be used to your advantage in understanding your partner. You will be much more discerning than most and therefore less likely to make mistakes that are difficult to rectify. You'll expect your partner to share in everything from cleaning the house to running a soup kitchen for the homeless, and to look good while he or she is doing it.

Your ideal lover will empathize with your humanitarian concerns and cope calmly with occasional eccentric behavior. He or she will also be family oriented, as you are, but he or she will need to understand that the day-to-day demands of parenthood can make you feel trapped.

Moon in Pisces

Those born when the Moon was in Pisces are the most compassionate and sensitive people of the zodiac. This extreme sensitivity is complicated by the dual Pisces nature and your occasional inexplicable changes of direction.

You are the world's greatest optimist, constantly wearing rose-colored glasses, and you always have a dream that something wonderful but unspecified is going to happen to you. You see it as your mission in life to help others, so you can be easily fooled by unscrupulous people who are out to use you for their own ends.

When this happens, you are deeply hurt, but you're more than likely to fall for the next sob story that comes along. In the same way, when one dream fails to materialize, you promptly replace it with another.

Your greatest dream is that one day you will find your true soul mate, the one person who is capable of fulfilling all your desires. This person will satisfy you intellectually, physically, and spiritually. You will be so much at one with this person that you will feel that you have known each other forever. Unfortunately, you are so anxious to love and be loved that you may choose the wrong partner. If this happens, you'll be devastated. You may even escape into your own fantasy world because you can't cope with the real one. It would be wiser to seek a period of seclusion or perhaps a retreat, until you feel able return to everyday life.

Beware of allowing your dream to take over your life so that it becomes one big romantic quest. With a Moon in Pisces, this is a real risk, as you do tend to wear your heart on your sleeve. Your craving for love is such that you can sometimes forget your usual reserve and actively pursue a person who attracts you. When the object of your pursuit is scared off by your enthusiasm, you're hurt, and the whole cycle begins again. Even then, you don't learn from experience. In this vulnerable state, you can be easily seduced into thinking that perhaps this time you have found the right partner, only to be disillusioned yet again.

Obviously, for you more than most, it's imperative to choose your lover with care. Your partner should appreciate your virtues, treat you like a precious object, and cherish you. One big advantage of your Moon in Pisces is that your instant recognition is likely to be mutual. You will feel a sense of homecoming, and all the past mistakes will seem like bad dreams. Before you commit yourself, though, be sure that this person can live up to your high ideals and that he or she will never let you down. Your partner must be able to lift you out of your mundane life, into that dream world you have sought for so long. Your beloved must also share your dreams and imaginative fantasies. For you, dreams are an essential part of life. With luck, your lover may be able to make some of them come true.

Rising Signs

Introduction

The rising sign, also known as the ascendant, is the zodiac sign that is rising above the eastern horizon at the moment of your birth. The Sun sign under which you were born is determined by the date. There are twelve zodiac signs; the Sun occupies each sign for approximately one month. Obviously, therefore, as long as you know your birthday, it is easy to determine your Sun sign.

Defining your rising sign is not quite so simple. There are twenty-four hours in a day, but only twelve signs in the zodiac wheel. This means that, generally speaking, the rising sign—that is, the one rising above the eastern horizon—changes every two hours. For this reason, you will need to know your time of birth in order to ascertain the rising sign.

Your rising sign concerns the persona you present to the world, how others see you, and how you establish your personality. Once you have defined your own ascendant, you will realize the importance of making similar discoveries about your potential partner. The rising-sign qualities superimpose themselves over the Sun-sign characteristics, rather like a transparent membrane through which you can still see what lies beneath.

The details below explain how you can determine the rising sign for yourself or anyone else in whom you are interested, as long as you have the time of birth.

The Rising-Sign Finder

The following system will work with reasonable accuracy wherever you were born, but please bear in mind that it is rough and ready, so if you want to be sure of your rising sign, you should contact an astrologer, or go to www.sashafenton.com.

How to do it

Read through this section while following the examples. The system will work as long as you have a reasonable idea of your time of birth. If you were born in a place and during a time when daylight saving or British summer time was in operation, you must deduct an hour from your time of birth.

Example 1

1.   Look at Figure 1, which has the time of day arranged around the edge. It looks like a clock face, but it shows the whole twenty-four hour day in two-hour blocks.

2.   Mark on the diagram the astrological symbol for the Sun (a circle with a dot in the middle). Place it in the segment corresponding to your time of birth. Our example shows someone born between 2 A.M. and 4 A.M.

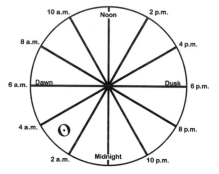

Figure 1

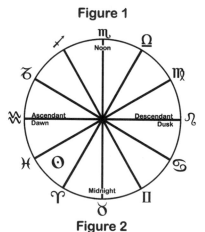

Figure 2

3. Place the name of your Sun sign on the line at the beginning of the block of time (counterclockwise) that your sun falls into. Figure 2 shows a person who was born between 2 A.M. and 4 A.M. under the sign of Pisces.

4. Write in the names of the other zodiac signs, in their correct order, counterclockwise around the chart.

5. The sign that appears on the left-hand side of the circle (in what would be the 9 o'clock position on an ordinary clock) is your rising sign. Figure 2 shows a person born with the Sun in Pisces and with Aquarius rising.

Example 2

Here is another example; this one is for a more awkward time of birth, being exactly on the line between two different blocks of time. This one is for a person born under the sign of Capricorn at 10 A.M.

1. The Sun is placed exactly on the 10 A.M. line.

2. The sign of Capricorn is placed on the 10 A.M. line.

3. All the other signs are placed in order (counterclockwise) around the chart.

4. This person has the sun in Capricorn and Pisces rising.

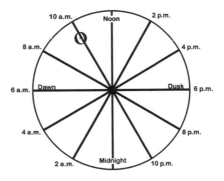

Figure 3

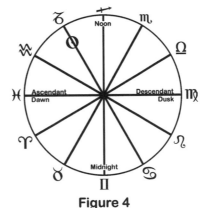

Figure 4

Your Rising Sign

Aries Rising

If Aries is your rising sign, other people will see you as a person of action. You have the enterprising spirit of an Arien, but without the brusqueness of those born with the Sun in Aries. Others look to you to initiate proceedings and get things done. You could be described as being pleasantly dynamic. You are kind and generous as well as possessing that desirable trait, a good sense of humor. Lacking the rough edge of the Aries Sun sign, you come across as cheerful and sassy, rather than abrasive and arrogant—traits that others willingly accept and which members of the opposite sex find most appealing.

Your forthright manner and complete honesty will endear you to your partner, who will know where things stand at all times. However, beware of being too brutally frank. An occasional little white lie can do wonders to smooth troubled waters and avoid impending disaster.

As soon as you crook your little finger, you'll expect your partner to come running, but he or she is not allowed to demand too much in return. You'll want to maintain your own interests outside the home and will expect your partner to follow his or her own hobbies, too. To you this seems a perfectly normal arrangement. There will be no jealousy on your part, and you won't expect any from your partner. Whichever your sex, you'll want your partner to take a fair share in the domestic chores or even more, if you can get away with it. You do need someone who can keep the house clean and tidy, as you consider such activities to be excluded from your duties.

Your chosen partner should have an intelligence that matches your own. In this respect, an Aries ascendant wants it both ways. You'd hate a partner who can outsmart you, but you need someone who can keep up with your intellectual standards. You don't want a partner who tries to make up your mind for you, though.

Anything that is predictable very quickly becomes boring for you. You expect your partner to provide variety in all things. As much as you might enjoy strawberries and cream, you wouldn't want to eat it every day. As another example, you'll want a full and varied sex life with a partner who has various desires and responses. You usually like to rush through life, but you're prepared to make an exception when you're in bed.

You love to be spoiled—whether by yourself or by others doesn't matter. In fact, Aries rising can be decidedly extravagant where his or her own interests are concerned. Male Aries rising would do well to remember that his partner, too, likes to be appreciated. You do tend to take it for granted that all's well and then wonder why your lover becomes irritable at times.

Taurus Rising

People who are seen by others to be stable in all respects will almost certainly have a Taurus ascendant. You approach everything with caution, never forging ahead until you have examined all aspects of the situation. Once your mind is made up, you'll give the undertaking your wholehearted attention, going ahead steadily at your own pace, in your own way, until you've achieved your goal. You hate to be rushed or pressurized either into making decisions or into taking practical action. This gives you an air of calm self-confidence that acts like a magnet to anyone in need of support. There are times when you feel that the whole world is relying on you for help. Be aware of this when looking for your partner. Make sure that you do the choosing. Otherwise, you may end up with someone who only wants to use you.

When it comes to forming a lasting connection, you'll need someone with whom you can have a truly deep relationship. Your Taurus ascendant ensures that you will feel this need at a much earlier age than most. You also need someone who will share your pleasures, anything from good food to fine art to satisfying sex. You like to indulge in all of these in equal measure and never hesitate to let your partner know.

Your chosen lover will swiftly recognize that persistence is another of your traits. Be careful to use this tenacity wisely; don't let it become pigheadedness. You have a tendency to stick with one idea to the exclusion of all else, and this can be a big mistake. When your partner's views differ from your own, be prepared to listen and be ready to give as well as take. You're not as lazy or possessive as someone with a Taurus Sun sign, but these traits may still form part of your personality. Your Taurus ascendant makes you more aware of this, and you will be careful to keep these unfavorable habits under control.

It won't trouble you if your partner is financially independent, because you admire a highflier. At the same time, you need to know where your partner is and will use your mobile phone to check on him or her. You can't bear your partner being away from you, leaving you in limbo until he or she returns. This attitude does not show lack of trust. You simply need to be able to visualize your partner at any given moment. It adds to your sense of security if you know where your chosen one is and what he or she is doing.

Finally, your ideal partner will be one with a touch of imagination, which is something you lack. You'll enjoy your life together much more if you allow yourself to broaden your outlook in this way.

Gemini Rising

With Gemini as your rising sign, you are regarded as a typical communicator. People see you as a witty, life-and-soul-of-the-party character. Beware that, in your attempts to live up to this image, you don't gossip too much. If you do, you may forget which story you've told to whom and get embarrassed. The problem is that your mind is forever jumping from one thought to the next. This is the fate of Gemini rising, because you are forever burdened with those twins, pulling in different directions. Most of the time, people will forgive your vagaries because they're beguiled by your dazzling sense of humor and ready wit, but you can also give the impression of being sarcastic and uncaring. As a result, you'll probably have many acquaintances but only a few true friends. This doesn't bother you because you're not the sort of person who needs or wants intimate friendships.

You're naturally curious and will probably have many lovers and a great deal of experience with partners before deciding that it's time to settle down. This may be later in life than the average, because you do enjoy playing the field. You also realize that complete commitment to just one person will mean that you won't always be in total control.

Your eventual choice of partner will certainly be someone lively and vivacious, who can also inspire you. This person won't need great emotional depth, and you shy away from too much sensitivity. Your wicked rapierlike tongue would devastate a sensitive person. You won't mind if your partner is slower than you are. In fact, you'll expect that and will enjoy becoming your partner's mentor.

Understanding is probably the most important quality for the partner of a Gemini ascendant. Those who don't know you well often regard you as cool and without passion. They are mistaken. You can be extremely competent in bed.

Does all this seem confused and contradictory? Sorry, but that's the way it is with a rising Gemini. You are a complex person who is difficult for others to understand, and you must consider this when choosing your partner.

Cancer Rising

If you have a Cancer ascendant, you will be known for your compassion and your ready response to the needs of others. Fortunately, you enjoy being surrounded by other people even if they do regard you mainly as the surrogate mother that all people need when they've lost their own. This is equally true for both sexes. It's also rather surprising in view of the fact that you carry with you your hard, crablike shell. At times, you may hide behind it, but this is usually only when you're hurt. That hard shell can be a convenient shelter, because you are easily upset. This supersensitivity leads to occasional introversion, and you're usually wary when meeting new people.

When you're looking for a partner, this wariness is intensified, and your approach is always indirect. Like the crab, you are incapable of making a head-on approach. Your advances are invariably circuitous, and you dread the moment when you actually come face to face. So why do you bother? The answer is because you cannot imagine a life in which you have to live alone.

If your chosen partner has already learned to trust and respect you, he or she may make the first approach, and this will be very much to your taste. Don't let your hard exterior get in the way. Forget your shell and let your natural emotional responses take over. Allow your reactions to come, as they surely will, from your heart rather than your head. Embrace your partner (metaphorically to start with) and take hom or her under your mother-hen wing. When this encounter takes place, you'll be able to relax and enjoy your partnership, reveling in the joy of loving and being loved.

Sex is probably of secondary importance to you. You'll prefer a quiet evening in, curled up with your lover on the sofa in front of a roaring fire. You're not averse to physical contact; just the reverse, in fact. However, the sort of body language you prefer is to walk home hand in hand and then sit entwined in peaceful silence.

Avoid making a commitment until you're convinced that your partner shares your philosophy of life. This may mean that they will be somewhat older than you are. This is probably an ideal scenario, as a younger person could put you under too much emotional stress. Your home needs to be a sanctuary in which you can relax in peace, mentally and physically. This is of primary importance, as any sort of pressure can reflect on your health, causing you to retreat completely into your shell. Your lover will understand this and, when you go for long walks alone, will recognize them as your safety valve.

Leo Rising

A Leo ascendant allows you to express your Sun sign characteristics much more authentically than would otherwise be the case. You'll be seen as positive and lighthearted, usually with a smile on your face. You will be much more kindhearted than a Sun-sign Leo and not needing to be in control of everything and everybody. You are something of a charismatic figure, always optimistic and bright. Your air of confidence gives the impression that there are no clouds to darken the horizon of your happy life. Is this true? You want others to recognize your superiority, admire you, and, above all, treat you with respect—hence the face you present to the world. In reality, you may well be beset with all sorts of hidden fears and doubts.

Your apparently carefree attitude makes you popular with the crowd, but your partner will need much more understanding of the real you. He or she will be aware of your weaknesses as well as your strengths and will be willing to accept them. Your partner will always be on hand with support and encouragement when needed. However, beware of flattery, particularly from those you have recently met. Some will take advantage of your generous nature when they realize that you can be manipulated.

Unfortunately, you seem to be drawn to people who want only a fleeting relationship. You may have discovered this the hard way early in life when you allowed yourself to be drawn into a relationship that failed dismally. If this is the case, you'll need to exercise particular care in selecting another partner.

You need someone who will support you come hell or high water. This person will be undisturbed by your lack of confidence and your other hidden fears. Furthermore, he or she will realize that any failure or humiliation could send you into a deep depression. You cannot bear to be mocked or ridiculed. If you're looking for a stable, long-term relationship, find someone who regards you with genuine respect and behaves accordingly. Loving and being loved is of primary importance to you, and your perfect partner will take care that you are always seen as the head of the household.

In return for your partner's consideration, check that your lover shares your pleasure in home comforts, pets, a wide circle of friends, interesting holidays, and a natural approach to enjoying the good life. Your partner should have a sense of humor, an optimistic outlook, and a graciousness that matches your own. With your optimism and faith in the future, you will eventually find your true love. When you do, any shadows will fall behind.

Virgo Rising

Your constant striving for self-improvement is typical of those with a Virgo ascendant. You possess a dignified, self-confident air, though others may think you remote and unfriendly. Little do they know that this facade conceals someone who is surprisingly shy. You can be suspicious and extremely critical. Any stranger with whom you hold a conversation will probably feel that he or she is being interrogated. You're emotionally cold and have difficulty in expressing your feelings.

None of these traits seem to be particularly attractive, but don't be too depressed. Some will see your quiet demeanor as being strong and laid-back. They may also find your shyness attractive. Accept this and don't be so diffident that you sell yourself short. Once you get talking about your pet subject, whatever it may be, you relax and your true nature begins to emerge. Be careful not to chitchat incessantly about your persnickety Virgo ways. Instead, enthusiastically share your vast store of knowledge on interesting topics. Once you've established some sort of rapport, your confidence will be boosted and you're on your way. What your partner won't realize is how much effort you have put into creating that initial contact.

If your relationship is to succeed, you must learn to live and let live. Try not to be critical of your partner. You'll have to learn to accept what you see as faults, or else abandon the idea that this person is for you. Bear in mind that you, too, have certain habits that it would be impossible for you to change. You will both have to agree on compromises if your relationship is to succeed, but do try to find someone who is at least reasonably orderly. An untidy partner will drive you crazy in twenty-four hours.

Your bashfulness, linked with your natural sexual urge, may lead you into making some terrible mistakes while you're still young. At that time, it's easy to confuse love with lust. If you slip up in this way, you could find yourself trapped in a wretched relationship. Being timid, you'll be unable to start over and look for a new partner. Instead, you'll remain in an unhappy situation and probably be unfaithful. This, in turn, will make you feel guilty and resentful.

To avoid this sort of mistake, take your time about getting to know any possible partner. Don't rush into any relationship if there is the remotest chance that you will regret it later. Be old-fashioned and insist on a long courtship, or be bold and put your cards on the table. Suggest a live-in romance with no formal commitment. If it works, you'll both be happy. If it doesn't, there will be no hard feelings. Above all, don't compromise your ideals—and remember that perfection exists only in the mind.

Libra Rising

If Libra is your ascendant, you'll give the impression of someone to whom peace and harmony are vital. Everything, like the Libra symbol of the scales, must be in balance. It's true that, deep down, you want your life to be all sweetness and light—but what are you going to do about it? The answer seems to be "as little as possible." Faced with any problem, you'll try to duck the issue and avoid having to make a decision. Like the ostrich with its head in the sand, you hope that if you don't recognize the problem it will go away, or someone else will solve it for you.

This may be an obstacle to finding happy relationships, but the opposite could be true, too. In view of your reluctance to deal with difficulties, a partner may be exactly what you need—someone prepared to take that burden off your shoulders. This could work out very well. Such an arrangement would provide the companionship you need. However, you should be very careful about the sort of person you invite to share your life.

Avoid anyone who is inflexible or jealous by nature. You will always require a fair amount of freedom and would resent having to account for your movements. You dislike discord and can usually see both sides of a question, which makes it difficult for anyone to quarrel with you. This means that unspoken inner resentment and frustration could come between you.

Beware of suddenly falling head over heels in love and convincing yourself that you've found your soul mate. In this situation, you may well commit yourself to what could turn out to be a disastrous experience. You may then indulge in a number of unsatisfactory affairs. On the other hand, if your partner is the one to leave, for whatever reason, you'll be devastated and determined never to trust anyone else, ever again.

Your very indecisiveness may be the characteristic that attracts the type of person who loves to help others—the perfect partner for you. This person will probably be carefree, lots of fun, and able to communicate with you on all levels. This partnership could be based on the attraction of opposites. Once the initial kinks have been ironed out, this pairing could give you the calm and balanced life you long for. For you, more than most, a stable and loving relationship is imperative if you are to have any success in life.

At the end of the day, and despite the fact that all astrology books harp on about Librans needing a partner, most of them end up on their own, and far happier than they ever were with the companionship of their partners.

Scorpio Rising

If Scorpio is your rising sign, you could well be seen by the rest of the world as something of a power freak. The term *laid back* is not in your vocabulary. What others don't realize is that your passion and intensity are used as a cover for your inner fears. You live in constant dread that someone or something will usurp your power and take control of your life. Perhaps this is the reason that you are so secretive, keeping your fears and feelings to yourself. Anyone who is acquainted with someone who has Scorpio rising will admit that they don't really know them at all.

You possess great energy and determination, and you will sweep aside any opposition. When things go wrong in your life, you react powerfully, starting all over again with strength and fortitude. You are highly intuitive and can decide in an instant whether something is black or white, right or wrong. Anything that fails to meet your high standards will be ruthlessly destroyed, and later rebuilt. Everything in your life is taken to extremes. To take but one example that is appropriate to our subject of partnerships— you will be either a skillful, insatiable lover or practically celibate, uninterested in sex. You may be an alcoholic or completely abstemious. You may be generous or penny-pinching. What's more, you will never, ever change your views about anything. Once you've reached a decision, you will stick with it, even if it means that you lose out heavily as a result.

You have extremely high standards of behavior and take intense pride in yourself, your work, and every other aspect of your life. Accepting criticism is difficult for you but, providing it is justified, you'll take the advice. However, you hate others to make fun of you and react savagely to jokes at your expense.

Not surprisingly, anyone with a Scorpio ascendant may have problems attracting the right partner. Some people may be intimidated by your intensity and air of mystery. Others will find you intriguing and charismatic and be drawn to you. You do have many good points, but you tend to hide them. The right person will bring out these virtues, recognizing you as loyal and loving, hardworking, and reliable. They will soon come to appreciate that you take all commitments seriously and that their trust will not be betrayed. One of your outstanding virtues is your complete loyalty.

No matter what problems beset your partner, your family, and your home, you will be there, offering support and strength.

Sagittarius Rising

If Sagittarius is your rising sign, other people are likely to be constantly astonished and even envious of your ability to lead a full life. You are never happier than when you're surrounded by people—the more the merrier. You want to be very involved with everything that is happening, and you are much in demand because of your enthusiasm and your ability to inspire others.

New ideas and projects always attract you. In fact, you always seem to be looking for something, but you probably don't know what that something is. The here and now is never good enough for you; you always need a challenge to look forward to. You may claim to be seeking freedom but, in fact, you are searching for your true self. Few people realize this, because you are the world's champion optimist, always happy and even-tempered.

However, what underlies this personality? Will you ever find what you are looking for? Do you really want to find it, or do you prefer to be a perpetual seeker? It's true that you often see opportunities that others miss, but you will quite happily abandon one grandiose scheme in favor of another when something more stimulating appears on the horizon. This is all the more extraordinary because you work hard at giving the impression that you're shrewd and successful. You are a never-ending source of exciting new ideas, but, with the best will in the world, you find it difficult to be reliable.

When it comes to relationships, you can be equally erratic. You make friends easily with a great variety of people, regardless of sex, race, creed, or color. You tend to seek out those who are different because they are the ones who interest you most. Thanks to your capricious nature, you have no hesitation in dropping friends when you have no further use for them, and that could mean that you make enemies. Those who have Sagittarius rising frequently prefer to have many friends and avoid serious commitments.

Yet in your heart you do want to love and be loved. You want a home where you can close the door, exclude the outside world, relax, and recharge your batteries with a loving and understanding partner. Lacking these essentials, you'll burn yourself out. You need someone who is attentive to your needs and able to offer consolation and comfort when needed. Above all else, that person should be openly demonstrative of his or her love for you.

Your need for love ensures that you won't be left on the shelf for long. You may, quite literally, grab a partner and heave a sigh of relief. If things don't work out, at least you won't break your heart and become a hermit. You'll shrug your shoulders and look for a replacement partner. In fact, you're not averse to a little two-timing, finding that two partners can be twice as comforting as one. Despite your devious nature, the fact remains that your family is the center of your life and your home is your haven when trouble strikes.

Capricorn Rising

This rising sign creates an impression of someone conventional and very predictable. You would no more dream of letting your hair down in public than you would of showing your true emotions. You will do all that you can to appear absolutely normal and not to cause comment or criticism. You're certainly unadventurous and, some would say, old-fashioned. You turn cold at even the possibility of making a fool of yourself, and embarrassing situations can literally paralyze you.

Yet behind this stiff and formal facade lurks someone who is very willing to be kind and friendly, if only you weren't so self-conscious and repressed. You're an ambitious person, willing to study and work hard in order to achieve your objectives. You have a sharp mind and may fly high in academic circles where you know you will be taken seriously. However, you lack endurance and will walk away from any project if it's not working out the way you expect.

You have little time for anything that is not already proven successful, and taking a gamble in any way would be out of the question for you. You need absolute security if you are ever to relax and enjoy life. Financial security, though not at the top of your agenda, is important. Without it, you tend to worry. Your biggest problems in life are certainly your lack of confidence and your inability to relate to other people. Both of these weaknesses make it difficult for you to establish a permanent relationship—though casual affairs are totally beyond your understanding.

You need a partner who is unassuming and protective and who shares your love of good food, music, and the arts. This person should be on your wavelength and able to provide the deep affection that you crave. Someone more gregarious than yourself would help you to lead a more balanced life. This person will also be ambitious, though probably in a field different from your own. He or she must certainly be prepared to work hard, for you despise laziness.

It will take a long time for your partner to get beyond the cold and formal face you present to the world and find the gentle, caring person beneath. You, too, will be wary about admitting your failings or showing the softer side of your character. Eventually, though, your partnership will blossom, quietly but with great intensity. You will never let your partner down, and the relationship could be happily permanent, just as long as your lover never makes you look foolish. If that happened, you would leave quietly, probably without a word of rebuke, with your confidence completely shattered. Strangely, though, this would not deter you from looking for another partner, preferably very different from the first.

Aquarius Rising

If Aquarius is your rising sign, you appear to be completely at ease with yourself and with the rest of the world. You seem to be a real cool dude and so easygoing that others may regard you as a pushover, which you're not. Nor are you as laid back as you appear. In fact, you're quite a nervous person, given to anxiety and worry, but you hide this behind what others think of as an air of self-importance.

When you come out with statements that are deliberately intended to shock, it's a big surprise to those who don't know you well. However, your friends will be aware that you delight in being outrageous. In this way, as in many others, you are completely unpredictable. Others may think you rude or thoughtless, but this is your way of stressing your eccentricity. You are fully aware of the quirks in your character and, at times, really struggle to behave as you know you should. You need to be in control of any situation in which you find yourself, and you believe that you and you alone are responsible for your own fate. When you do make mistakes, you are unperturbed and accept full responsibility with your usual nonchalance.

Once you have made a promise, you'll be sure to honor it; it is not in your nature to abandon either a project or a partner once you've made a commitment. This can lead to problems when you have been too fanciful in your ambitions. Your partner won't be happy if you're unable to differentiate between your dreams and reality. However, he or she will be grateful for your dependability and kindness. For some reason, though, this kindness doesn't extend to being charitable to anyone who has a minor health complaint. You're compassion itself with anyone who is ill, but you lose patience with people who feel sorry for themselves.

You have a naturally friendly disposition and enjoy making new acquaintances. They quickly relax in your company, charmed by your ready wit and humor. This gives you a head start when it comes to looking for a partner. Without realizing it, you will attract fiery, passionate people who will balance your own easygoing style.

Your perfect partner must be quick-minded in order to keep up with you, and independent, so that you can maintain your freedom. Because you are not a demonstrative person, you will prefer your partner not to be overeffusive. You will probably choose someone who is quite a few years younger than yourself and who is a cut above the average in many ways. You'll want someone good-looking, warm, and friendly, but equally important, someone who appreciates your spiritual interests and can share them. Overall, your requirements constitute a pretty tall order—but you could be lucky in love.

Pisces Rising

Anyone with Pisces rising will sometimes escape into a fantasy world when things go wrong. At the same time, you are compassionate and caring, easily able to empathize with others, appreciate their problems, and offer practical help. However, you are quite unpredictable and liable to change your perceived identity from one minute to the next. Small wonder that you totally confuse people who are more down-to-earth.

Fortunately, you don't allow your impulsive nature to interfere with your ambition. If asked, you'd say that above all else you want to be a success. What you wouldn't say is that you also want to understand the deeper meaning of life. This sensitivity, allied to your compassionate nature, often means that you worry unnecessarily.

Pisces rising has one trait that always confuses other people, as you can feel two conflicting emotions at the same time. You may seem to be in a rage about something that has upset you when you are really quite placid, but conversely, you can appear to be unconcerned when, in fact, you are seething underneath. It's all part of your Piscean nature, with the two fish linked but pulling in different directions.

Beware of parasites who try to hook on to you solely for what they can get. Your trusting, preoccupied air makes them think they can take advantage of you. Fortunately, you're not such a simpleton as they think and you are quite astute, with an amazing understanding of others. You can notice subtleties that others miss and, in conversation, quickly notice when the words spoken differ from the thoughts behind them.

All these attributes will help when it comes to choosing a partner. The one you are looking for should be as shrewd as you are and supportive of you and your endeavors. You'll also need someone who can accept your laid-back, tolerant attitude, and share your love of animals. When you do settle down in a stable relationship, your loving twosome wouldn't be complete without at least one pet.

It's quite possible that you won't find your ideal partner easily; you may make mistakes along the way. You may be drawn into a relationship that seems right at the time but turns out to be a case of you giving and the other person taking. An early encounter like this is often the result of mistaking lust for love. You'll put up with this for a while but, when you recognize that things are not going to improve, you'll draw a line through that relationship and move on.

Look for a partner who makes no secret of their devotion, shares your interests, communicates well, and can provide you with a peaceful home life.

Index